Floating Exchange Rates and International Monetary Reform

Floating Exchange Rates and International Monetary Reform

Thomas D. Willett

American Enterprise Institute for Public Policy Research
Washington, D.C.

Thomas D. Willett is Horton Professor of Economics at Claremont Graduate School and Claremont Men's College.

Library of Congress Cataloging in Publication Data

Willett, Thomas D
    Floating exchange rates and international monetary reform.

    (AEI studies ; 172)
    1. Foreign exchange problem. 2. International finance. I. Title. II. Series: American Enterprise Institute for Public Policy Research. AEI studies ; 172.
HG3821.W53   332.4′5   77-13327
ISBN 0-8447-3271-0

AEI studies 172

Printed in the United States of America

CONTENTS

4   **INTERNATIONAL SURVEILLANCE OF THE
    ADJUSTMENT PROCESS UNDER
    FLOATING RATES**   109

5   **SUMMARY AND CONCLUSIONS**   135

PREFACE

The debate over fixed versus flexible exchange rates has long been dear to the hearts of economists. But for many years this subject was widely viewed as being only of academic interest. A decade ago "fixed" exchange rates were viewed by most monetary officials as being the backbone of international financial cooperation and the stability of the international monetary system. Floating exchange rates were viewed as being beyond the realm of consideration by men of practical affairs. Today, almost all of the major industrial countries have floating currencies, albeit with varying degrees of official management.

At Kingston, Jamaica, in early 1976 representatives of the over 100 member nations of the International Monetary Fund reached agreement on Amendments to the IMF Articles of Agreement which in substance officially ratified floating rates as the basis for our international monetary system. How did such a substantial shift in views come about, and how solid a foundation do floating rates provide for our international monetary system? Were the Jamaica Agreements just a stopgap measure and are further basic international monetary reforms urgently needed as some critics have charged?

In this study I have attempted to address such questions against the background of a historical review of academic and official views on exchange rate arrangements and the establishment and evolution of the postwar international monetary system. These topics have been my major area of professional concern for the past decade, both as an academic at Cornell, Harvard, and the University of Virginia and in government service as senior staff economist at the Council of Economic Advisers and as deputy assistant secretary for international research and planning and director of international monetary research at the U.S. Treasury.

This study was written while the author was director of international monetary research at the U.S. Treasury Department, but the views expressed are solely those of the author and do not necessarily reflect those of the U.S. government. In its preparation I have accumulated a large number of debts. Without implying their necessary agreement with all of the conclusions of the study, I should like to thank: Jacob Dreyer, George Halm, Steven Kohlhagen, John Makin, Frank McCormick, Charles Pigott, John Rutledge, Wilson Schmidt, Marie Thursby, Ed Tower, Ted Truman, Marina Whitman, John Williamson, George Willis, and, especially, Sven Arndt, Richard Sweeney, and Gottfried Haberler for reading and commenting on various parts of the manuscript. Excellent typing and research assistance from Norman Carleton, Craig Larimer, Barbara McBride, Dion Reich, and Brigita Woods is gratefully acknowledged. I should also like to thank my family for their patience and understanding during the evening and weekend hours devoted to the study.

1

INTRODUCTION: FROM BRETTON WOODS TO JAMAICA

It is not possible to date precisely the end of the international monetary system established at Bretton Woods in 1944. Different aspects of the system died at different times. And the basic principles of international financial cooperation on which the Bretton Woods system was based never died at all.

There is general agreement that the final end of the adjustably pegged par value exchange rate system established at Bretton Woods was marked by the initiation of generalized floating of exchange rates by the major industrial countries following the second devaluation of the dollar in early 1973. But many who viewed the gold convertibility of the dollar as the linchpin of the system would point to the formal termination of the convertibility of official dollar holdings into gold in August 1971 as the symbolic death date of the system. Still others would point out that, de facto, the unfettered gold convertibility of the dollar as envisioned at Bretton Woods had already ended years before.

This study reviews the role of exchange rate arrangements and proposals for their reform in the evolution of the international monetary system and analyzes how the adoption of floating rates provided the foundation for the comprehensive reform of the international monetary system at Jamaica in 1976. While it is appropriate to speak of our having a new international monetary system in many basic respects, our new system is one clearly evolved out of the Bretton Woods arrangements. Although there are many differences in the procedures and mechanisms of our new system, the valuable aspects of its parentage have been maintained, especially the spirit and traditions of international financial cooperation as opposed to economic isolationism. It is difficult to overemphasize the importance which the adoption of the liberal economic philosophy of Bretton Woods

1

has had in stimulating the postwar growth and prosperity of the world economy. This study thus begins with a review of the negotiations that culminated in the establishment of our postwar international monetary system.

Bretton Woods and the Par Value System

The negotiations that established our postwar international monetary system at Bretton Woods, New Hampshire, in 1944, were heavily influenced by a desire not to repeat the major mistakes of the interwar period.[1] Indeed this sense of history dominated postwar economic planning in general and explains why so much attention was paid to such planning while still in the middle of the war. President Roosevelt and Secretary of State Cordell Hull were both convinced that much of the disaster of the interwar period and even the precipitation of World War II itself stemmed from failure to include economic considerations as a major aspect of post-World War I planning. They were determined not to repeat this mistake.[2] Nor was Lord Keynes, the chief British negotiator, unmindful of the lessons of the interwar period.

To most of the Bretton Woods negotiators these lessons in the international monetary area were threefold. The increased concern with freedom to use domestic macroeconomic policies for full employment ruled out a return to a gold standard or any other system of genuinely fixed rates. Keynes was particularly influenced by the disastrous effects of the British decision to restore the prewar gold parity of the pound in 1923.[3] Likewise the 1920s and 1930s were also thought to have demonstrated the undesirability of both freely floating exchange rates and of an independently managed adjustable peg system. In this regard, Ragnar Nurkse's major study for the League of Nations on international currency[4] reflected widely held academic

---

[1] For discussion of the Bretton Woods negotiations, see A. L. K. Acheson, J. F. Chant, and M. F. J. Prachonney, eds., *Bretton Woods Revisited* (Toronto: University of Toronto Press, 1972); Alfred E. Eckes, *A Search For Solvency: Bretton Woods and the International Monetary System, 1941–1971* (Austin: University of Texas Press, 1976); Richard N. Gardner, *Sterling-Dollar Diplomacy: The Origins and the Prospects of Our International Economic Order*, rev. ed. (New York: McGraw-Hill, 1969); Roy F. Harrod, *The Life of John Maynard Keynes* (New York: Harcourt Brace, 1951); and David Rees, *Harry Dexter White* (New York: Coward, McCann and Geoghigan, 1973).

[2] See, for example, Eckes, *A Search for Solvency*, pp. 1, 21. See also Cordell Hull, *The Memoirs of Cordell Hull*, 2 vols. (New York: MacMillan, 1948).

[3] See, for example, Harrod, *Life of John Maynard Keynes*, chap. 9.

[4] Ragnar Nurkse, *International Currency Experience: Lessons of the Inter-war Period* (New York: United Nations, 1947), reprint of the original League of Nations edition published in 1944.

views at that time and was extremely influential in further spreading these views.

It should be noted that Nurkse, unlike many postwar critics of floating rates, was careful to point out that the widespread beggar-thy-neighbor policies of the 1930s were not carried out under a regime of floating rates but one of adjustably pegged rates.[5] The tendency of some postwar critics to identify floating with the beggar-thy-neighbor policies of the 1930s reflected a gross ignorance of history. The distrust of freely floating rates by informed economists of the time was based rather on the experiences of the 1920s. During this period of extensive floating there was indeed considerable exchange rate volatility and at times massive flows of speculative and flight capital. The accepted interpretation at the time as presented in Nurkse's study was that these were evidences of the frequently destabilizing or disequilibrating nature of capital flows and the undesirability of floating rates. Nurkse concluded that

> any system of exchange rates reached by international consultation will be better than one in which exchanges are determined either by isolated acts of national sovereignty or by markets subject to speculative transfers of funds. To let the exchanges "find their own level" would almost certainly result in chaos.
>
> . . . If there is anything that inter-war experience has clearly demonstrated, it is that paper currency exchanges cannot be left free to fluctuate from day to day under the influence of market supply and demand.[6]

Typical of the view widely held at the time is the following quotation from Gottfried Haberler's important 1945 article on the choice of exchange rates after the war:

> it is certain that a system of "free exchanges" would lead to extremely undesirable results. It would incite capital flight and violent fluctuations. There are very few instances of really free exchanges in monetary history and none that could be called successful.[7]

Later research has raised serious questions about the soundness of this interpretation of the interwar experiences with floating.[8] At

---

[5] Ibid., p. 8.

[6] Ibid., p. 137.

[7] Gottfried Haberler, "The Choice Of Exchange Rates After the War," *American Economic Review*, vol. 35, no. 3 (June 1945), pp. 308–18.

[8] See, for example, Leland B. Yeager, *International Monetary Relations* (New York: Harper and Row, 1966), and the references cited there. A useful recent

that time, economists generally failed to distinguish between volatility in capital flows and exchange rates as a reflection of underlying economic, financial, and political instability on the one hand, and speculation as an independent cause of instability on the other. Indeed, the conventional terminology of that day referred to capital flows as equilibrating and disequilibrating purely on the basis of whether they tended to move the exchange rate or keep it constant; in other words, whether they moved in the same or opposite directions to changes in the other components of the balance of payments. But, as Friedman argued in his classic 1950 article on flexible exchange rates,[9] this is not really an economic but a statistical definition. The economist's normal usage of equilibrating and disequilibrating refers to whether a movement toward or away from "equilibrium" is caused. Thus, where one country is inflating more rapidly than another, for instance, a depreciation of its exchange rate, at least up to some amount, should be viewed as equilibrating rather than disequilibrating. Attempts to reinterpret the interwar experience with floating, taking into account this distinction, have been inevitably somewhat inconclusive, as it is impossible to determine unambiguously what the equilibrium rate really was at any point in time. Nevertheless, the results of this more recent research indicate that many of the major episodes of exchange rate volatility during this period can be explained largely in terms of the underlying economic and political instabilities and uncertainties of the time, and that major episodes of genuinely destabilizing speculation, if they did exist, were the exception rather than the general rule.

But widespread recognition of this awaited advances in economic analysis. At the time of Bretton Woods, academic and official views were largely in congruence on the issue of floating rates and there was little debate about the form of the exchange rate system which was adopted.[10] As George Halm has reported:

> The monetary experts who participated in the great debate preceding the Bretton Woods Conference of 1944 were opposed to both permanently fixed and freely floating exchange rates. The nearly complete silence of proponents of

---

review of the interwar experience is given in Gottfried Haberler, *The World Economy, Money and the Great Depression, 1919–1939* (Washington, D.C.: American Enterprise Institute, 1976).

[9] Milton Friedman, "The Case for Flexible Exchange Rates," in *Essays in Positive Economics* (Chicago: University of Chicago Press, 1953), pp. 157–203.

[10] This is a surprising revelation to someone such as myself who began his study of international financial questions in the 1960s when strong differences had developed between academic and official views.

this form of flexibility [floating] excluded the system from discussion.[11]

A system was sought that would recognize that exchange rates were a question of international as well as purely national concern and that would avoid the extremes of both permanently fixed and freely floating rates. In general, economists of the period began with a predisposition toward fixed rates, which had been the majority view of both classical and neoclassical economists. But they recognized that defense of a parity could become unjustifiably costly, in the face of the development of a serious underlying disequilibrium, and that in such instances, the exchange rate rather than domestic macroeconomic policies should be adjusted.[12]

These views on exchange rates were shared by the leading critic of the Bretton Woods approach to international monetary organization, John H. Williams of Harvard University, and the Federal Reserve Bank of New York. Williams was the originator of the so-called key currency approach to monetary reform, which received considerable support in the New York financial community.[13] The thrust of Williams's approach was that because of the vast differences in the economic structures and situations of different countries and the need for substantial adjustments to the dislocation of the war, the universalistic approach of the Bretton Woods reformers was unrealistic. Williams advocated instead a more pragmatic approach based on cooperation among the major industrial countries. He argued

that the problem of international monetary stability is primarily that of maintaining a state of proper economic health

---

[11] George Halm, The "Band" Proposal: The Limits of Permissable Exchange Rate Variations, Princeton Special Papers in International Economics, no. 6 (January 1965), pp. 1, 2. Halm cites as an exception the arguments of Mr. Benson in the British parliamentary debate on the International Clearing Union. See also Halm, The International Monetary Fund and Flexibility of Exchange Rates, Princeton Essays in International Finance, no. 83 (March 1971), pp. 4, 5, where he cites criticism by Frank Graham and R. G. Hawtrey.

[12] Early twentieth-century critics of the gold standard such as Keynes, Frank Graham, and Irving Fisher, agreed that in cases of a serious conflict, the question was whether domestic policy or exchange rates should be adjusted. As Harrod puts it, "The question for him [Keynes] was whether our currency should be managed so as to secure stable external value, i.e., to maintain a fixed dollar parity (so-called Gold Standard), or whether it should be managed so as to secure a stable internal price level. His decision was in favor of the latter" (The Life of John Maynard Keynes, pp. 400–01). Nor did Nurkse favor permanently fixed rates. See Nurkse, International Currency Experience, pp. 211–12.

[13] Most of Williams's writings on this subject are conveniently collected in John H. Williams, Post War Monetary Plans and Other Essays, third edition (New York: Alfred A. Knopf, 1947).

in the leading countries; and that this is the only workable answer to the whole conflict between internal and external monetary stability, about which discussions of the gold standard for years revolved. This means collaboration to maintain both a high level of real income within the leading countries and a high degree of exchange stability between them. If this could be done, the problem of maintaining exchange stability for the other countries, and a reasonable state of economic well being within them, would probably not present major problems.[14]

While Williams's key currency approach was not accepted as the basis for our postwar international monetary system, it did at times have important effects on the manner in which the system was operated in practice. One can also note a striking similarity between Williams's key currency approach and the philosophy of the recent Rambouillet and Jamaica agreements discussed in chapter 3. Despite his strong differences in institutional approach to postwar monetary arrangements, Williams was in substantial agreement with the Bretton Woods negotiators on exchange rate procedures. While opposing freely floating rates, Williams was also skeptical of rigid rates and argued strongly for the desirability of compromise arrangements.[15]

While the form of exchange rate flexibility to be incorporated into the Bretton Woods arrangements was not a major subject of debate, there was discussion of how much of a matter of last resort exchange rate adjustments should be. In this regard there was definite evolution in the thinking of the major participants in the negotiations toward support for greater flexibility in the use of parity adjustments. Harry Dexter White, the chief U.S. negotiator, seems to have been less sympathetic to frequent exchange rate adjustments than were the British negotiators. Keynes's views changed considerably as the prospective size of the lending capacity of the International Monetary Fund became clearer. Keynes's initial preference had been for large scale financing of payments imbalances with more limited use of exchange rate adjustments. As it became clear that much smaller quantities of funds would be available for financing, Keynes saw the need for a corresponding increase in the frequency with which exchange rate adjustments were used.[16] Unfortunately,

---

[14] Ibid., p. 19.

[15] Ibid., especially pp. 199–227.

[16] For example, John H. Williams described the 1944 draft statement of experts which presented a compromise of the Keynes and White plans published in 1943

however, as is reviewed in the following sections, it proved difficult to apply in practice the greater propensity to adjust exchange rates intended by the Bretton Woods negotiators.

The Overlooked Problem: Speculative Capital Flows under an Adjustable Peg System

Relatively little attention appears to have been paid by the Bretton Woods negotiators to the question of exactly how such exchange rate adjustments should be made. As Harrod has described their thinking, both "Keynes and White agreed that it was desirable to have a fixed rate of exchange in the short run, with flexibility in the long run."[17] Thinking of the issue in this way makes it easier to gloss over the fact that such long-run flexibility can only occur by adjustments in some future short runs. The difficulties associated with making such adjustments were largely overlooked. But of course it is much easier to criticize this crucial omission with hindsight than it would have been at the time.

As seen by the participants in the negotiations, the main exchange rate issue, and it certainly was a crucial one, was the relative roles of national authorities and the international community in initiating and approving exchange rate adjustments. And by far the greatest opposition to the Bretton Woods exchange rate arrangements came from advocates of a return to the gold standard and permanently fixed rates, rather than advocates of floating exchange rates.[18] It was primarily the advocates of floating rates such as Frank Graham who raised questions about the workability of an adjustable peg system, but little attention appears to have been paid to criticisms from such sources.

---

in the following manner: "Much the most significant part of the new draft is the section on exchange rates ... Clearly, substantially greater exchange rate variability is contemplated in the new draft, and one does not need a seat at the official experts' table to recognize that this is Britain's main rejoinder to the decision to adopt a stabilization fund of moderate size and with limited American commitment, as against their original proposal for a very large clearing union" (Williams, *Post-War Monetary Plans*, p. 1).

[17] Harrod, *The Life of John Maynard Keynes*, p. 641.

[18] For example, the *New York Times* advocated a return to the gold standard and Jacob Viner, perhaps the leading international economist at that time, criticized the Bretton Woods arrangement for allowing too much exchange rate flexibility. On the range of reactions, see Eckes, *A Search for Solvency*, chaps. 4 and 7. It was then common to refer to any type of exchange rate system other than permanently fixed rates as a form of flexible exchange rates. Of the many possible types of flexible rates, floating was widely considered to be the most extreme and undesirable.

7

In his cogent article in the *American Economic Review* in 1940, Graham pointed out that when confidence in an adjustably pegged exchange rate system deteriorated, the direction of any change would be clear and "bear speculators are then presented with that rare, and greatly desired phenomenon, a 'sure thing'."[19] However, despite the fact that Graham occupied one of the most prestigious academic chairs in the country, his paper, which was published in the foremost economic journal, seems to have had little impact on the negotiations, or in the academic literature of the time, in attracting either support or opposition.[20]

Another factor that diverted serious attention from the speculative problems associated with an adjustably pegged par value system was the common assumption that capital controls would be widely maintained for the indefinite future. Such controls were apparently the mechanism by which the adjustable peg was to be made workable. Lutz argued that, by establishing the conditions for riskless speculation,

> The Keynes scheme, in consequence, simply invites short-term capital movements. The author, it is true, suggests a control of them, without, however, making such control an integral part of his scheme. We shall later indicate that the introduction of the control of capital movements is no easy or pleasant matter. In view of this fact, it seems more reasonable to provide from the outset that the nature of a

---

[19] Frank Graham, "Achilles' Heels in Monetary Standards," *American Economic Review*, vol. 20, no. 1, pt. 1 (March 1940), pp. 16–32. Graham himself advocated some official management of floating rates, especially to "punish" bear speculators. As Graham described his position, he advocated a "policy of reasonably flexible exchange rates with the deliberate intent of punishing noxious speculation" (p. 23). He noted that "The border of the zone should therefore be not sharply defined and the zone itself should be somewhat wider than that which Mr. Keynes has espoused" (p. 23). Likewise, in an analysis anticipating the articles that would advocate flexible exchange rates a decade or more later, he argued that "... it seems probable that freely flexible rates would give greater underlying stability than attends the attempt to maintain rigid rates, since the latter are, in fact, punctuated by sizable breaks" (p. 28).

[20] One of the few other criticisms at that time of the adjustable peg aspect of the Bretton Woods proposals was raised by Friedrich Lutz, who was with Graham at Princeton, *The Keynes and White Proposals*, Princeton Essays in International Finance, no. 1 (July 1943). Another instance was the quite interesting article by Lowell M. Pumphrey, "The Exchange Equalization Account of Great Britain, 1932–1939: Exchange Operations," *American Economics Review*, vol. 32, no. 4 (December 1942), pp. 803–16. Pumphrey takes basically the same view as Graham.

currency in terms of Bancor [Keynes' proposed new international reserve] will be allowed to fluctuate within certain limits.[21]

After detailing many disadvantages of controls, including their effects in undermining business ethics, Lutz concluded that "the only sound method of preventing short-term capital movements of the speculative and political kind is to remove their causes."[22] Such good advice fell on deaf ears, however.

Frequently not realized today is the degree of suspicion with which many of the Bretton Woods negotiators regarded international capital flows and the extent to which they anticipated continued heavy reliance on capital controls in the postwar period. The conventional wisdom of that time exaggerated the distinction between the benefits of free trade and those of free capital flows and also how much the latter could be controlled without affecting the former. As Louis Rasminsky has described the expectations of the negotiators at Bretton Woods: "We did not foresee the extent to which exchange controls would be abolished after the war. The articles of agreement of the Fund are friendly to the idea of exchange control. It was practically assumed that there will be exchange controls on capital."[23]

In large part the distrust of liquid capital flows reflected the misinterpretation of the experiences of the interwar period, which were thought to have discredited floating rates. It is also interesting to note that the two chief negotiators had both written major attacks on the view that freedom of international long-term capital flows was in the national interests of capital-exporting countries.[24]

Keynes argued in his proposals for an international clearing union that

> There is no country which can, in future, safely allow the flight of funds for political reasons or to evade taxation or anticipation of the owner turning refugee. . . .

---

[21] Lutz, *The Keynes and White Proposals*, p. 13.

[22] Ibid., p. 19.

[23] Louis Rasminsky et al., "Canadian Views," in Acheson et al., *Bretton Woods Revisited*.

[24] See J. M. Keynes, "The Future of the Foreign Exchanges," *Lloyds Bank Monthly Review* (December 1935), pp. 67–74, and Harry D. White, *The French International Accounts, 1880–1913* (Cambridge: Harvard University Press, 1933), chaps. 12–14. White concludes that "The study of French foreign investments supports, in my opinion, the growing belief that capital exports are not always beneficial to the exporting country and that some measure of intelligent control of the volume and direction of foreign investments is desirable" (pp. 311–12).

. . . For these reasons it is widely held that control of capital movements, both inward and outward, should be a permanent feature of the postwar system.[25]

Keynes recognized that to be effective such controls would probably require exchange controls for all transactions, trade as well as capital. He argued that he was not against international investment per se and that such a system of controls "should greatly facilitate the restoration of international loans and credits for legitimate purposes";[26] rather such a system would be designed to control "short term speculative movements or flights of currency."[27] In his article, "The Future of the Foreign Exchanges," Keynes also advocated a "strict, though not pedantic, control of the rate of new foreign lending," because, "Only by this means can a country maintain sufficient autonomy over the domestic rate of interest."[28]

Nurkse argued in similar vein that

one need not contemplate the future as if . . . all international movements of private funds would have to be severely restricted or prevented altogether. What may have to be prevented are the massive one-way movements, usually self-aggravating in character, which serve no useful social function and which may wreck any orderly system of international monetary relations.[29]

Development of the False Identification of the Par Value System with International Financial Cooperation

Recognition of this view of the world and the priority of issues held at Bretton Woods makes the adoption of the par value, adjustable peg system of exchange rate arrangements at Bretton Woods much more understandable than when seen from the perspective of the high capital mobility of the past decade. Indeed, the postwar international monetary system based on the par value exchange rate system was remarkably successful in avoiding the disastrous competitive depreciations and beggar-thy-neighbor trade restrictions of

---

[25] John M. Keynes, "Proposals for an International Clearing Union," reprinted in Herbert G. Grubel, ed., *World Monetary Reform* (Stanford: Stanford University Press, 1963), p. 72.

[26] Ibid., p. 73.

[27] Ibid., p. 74.

[28] Keynes, "The Future of the Foreign Exchanges," p. 71.

[29] Nurkse, *International Currency Experience*, p. 189.

the 1930s, and in the earlier part of the postwar period it contributed to an unprecedented expansion of world trade and economic prosperity.

It is not surprising that to many the exchange rate procedures adopted at Bretton Woods became a symbol of international financial cooperation, rather than just the form in which such cooperation was initially implemented. For many people pegged exchange rates and the par value system became falsely identified with internationalism, the rule of law, and international financial cooperation; while greater exchange rate flexibility became equally falsely associated with isolationism, destructive economic nationalism, international anarchy, and all of the many disorders of the 1930s.

As a result of this false identification of particular exchange rate procedures with much broader principles of the conduct of national policies, many feared that the widespread abandonment of the par value system in 1973 would lead to a repeat of such antisocial behavior.[30] And even after generalized floating had successfully avoided an outbreak of such policies for several years in spite of all the additional international economic and financial problems associated with the huge increases in the price of oil, many continued to fear that an outbreak of such policies lurked just around the corner.

The threat of widespread beggar-thy-neighbor policies is, of course, not something to be taken lightly. But recent experience suggests that the actual operation of the postwar international monetary system has evolved to the point where the framework of international financial cooperation and the principle of avoiding blatant beggar-thy-neighbor policies can be clearly separated from the specific set of exchange rate arrangements or procedures in force. The most important aspect of the Bretton Woods Agreements was the decision of the major countries to follow a basic course of multilateralism, liberal economic policies, and international cooperation (albeit with many exceptions), rather than the alternative of heavy emphasis on bilateralism, trade restrictions, and go-it-alone nationalism.

This point was well put by Ansel Luxford, the top Treasury lawyer in the American delegation at Bretton Woods, in a letter to Richard Gardner.

> To me, then as now, the major significance of Bretton Woods
> was the death blow it represented in victory over economic

---

[30] For further discussion on this point, see Thomas D. Willett, "Our Evolving International Economic System," in *The Changing International Economic Order* (Charlottesville: University of Virginia Press, forthcoming).

isolationism of the pre-war period and the serious threat that with military victory this country would again revert to economic nationalism. Thus, the question of how effective the Bank and Fund may have been in the light of post-war events (many of them not foreseeable except with hindsight) is not nearly so important as having established the principle of U.S. cooperation in the solution of the international economic problems of the future.[31]

Indeed, this is why one can confidently point to Bretton Woods as a most significant success for international monetary relations despite the fact that the International Monetary Fund was relatively inactive for most of its first decade, with little actual use made of many of the procedures negotiated at Bretton Woods. Much of the overshadowing of the Fund as an instrument of international financial cooperation during this period was due to the large British Loan and Marshall Plan aid granted directly by the United States; but as Luxford went on to point out in his letter to Gardner, the ground for these actions was laid at Bretton Woods by "having established the principle of U.S. cooperation and having obtained public acceptance thereof."[32]

The heart of Bretton Woods was in its principles, not its procedures. Likewise, the importance of the monetary institution created at Bretton Woods, the International Monetary Fund, has been much greater than would be implied by the direct actions of the Fund alone. As Louis Rasminsky, one of the chief Canadian negotiators at Bretton Woods, has pointed out:

> One of the results of the establishment of the Fund that has not received enough emphasis is the great increase in international consultation and collaboration. This seems so obvious that it may seem jejune even to mention it, but to those of us who saw what international cooperation in these matters was like before the war the difference is tremendous.[33]

At the time of Bretton Woods, a clear distinction between exchange rate procedures and basic principles of international economic cooperation may well not have been practical. One can make a

---

[31] Quoted in Richard N. Gardner, "The Political Setting," in Acheson et al., *Bretton Woods Revisited*, p. 32.

[32] Ibid., p. 33.

[33] Ibid., p. 37. See also Edward M. Bernstein, "The Evolution of the International Monetary System," in this same volume, pp. 51–65.

reasonable, although not conclusive, case that, under the circumstances, the exchange rate arrangements at Bretton Woods were a wise choice that substantially reduced the risk of a repeat of the 1930s and nurtured financial cooperation. But the need for a par value system has declined as the postwar monetary system has evolved, while at the same time the disadvantages of this set of procedures have multiplied rapidly.

The Breakdown of the Par Value System

The three major factors underlying the growing disadvantages of the adjustable peg were (1) the extreme reluctance to make use of the provision to adjust exchange rates, (2) the greater speed and magnitude with which balance-of-payments disequilibrium began to emerge at constant exchange rates, and (3) larger international movements of capital in response to perceived disequilibrium in exchange rates and consequent expectations of exchange rate changes. By discouraging exchange changes except as a measure of last resort, the Bretton Woods exchange rate arrangements united both strong economic and political incentives against using such measures, and for a period during the 1950s and 1960s, Bretton Woods became virtually a fixed rate system.[34]

It was not genuinely a fixed rate system, however. Countries were not willing to accept the requirement of such a system that monetary and other macroeconomic policies be geared to the dictates of balance-

---

[34] A good discussion of these biases is given in Stephen Marris, *The Bürgenstock Communique*, Princeton Essays in International Finance, no. 89 (May 1970), pp. 13–35. A study by Richard Cooper, *Currency Devaluation in Developing Countries*, Princeton Essays in International Finance, no. 86 (June 1971), suggests that in short-run political terms finance ministers were well-advised to try strenuously to avoid devaluation. In Cooper's sample, the turnover of finance ministers who had presided over devaluation was considerably above average. There is some disagreement in the literature as to how much this bias against exchange rate adjustments was an inevitable consequence of the Bretton Woods exchange rate system and how much it was the result of the particular views of leading international financial officials and the consequent types of policies followed under the adjustable peg system during the 1940s and early to mid-1960s; in other words, whether the difficulty was not with particular policies rather than with the system. My own guess would be that the nature of the exchange rate system and the set of attitudes governing the operation of the system over this period were both important independent factors, either one of which would have been sufficient to undermine the workings of the system. But whatever the reasons, it is clear that, as Rasminsky has indicated, the Bretton Woods negotiators "did not foresee the reluctance that governments would have to adjust the adjustable peg" ("Canadian Views," in Acheson et al., *Bretton Woods Revisited*). Rasminsky mentions both the unforeseen increases in international capital mobility and in inflation as reasons for the reluctance to depreciate.

of-payments equilibria. Thus, attempts to maintain par values increasingly took the form of combinations of various types of controls and special financial measures. In attempts to ward off speculative capital flows, national officials would tend to offer assurances that changes in the rate would not be made, thus converting maintenance of the rate to an important political objective of the officials who had made such promises. Decisions to adjust exchange rates were delayed further by the tendency to hope that autonomous payments developments would reverse and/or that other countries would take steps to correct mutual imbalances.

As long as differences in underlying economic and financial conditions developed only slowly and the response of capital flows to views that exchange rates were out of line remained fairly small, then the adverse effects of insufficient use of exchange rate adjustments were not highly visible. As the postwar period progressed, however, a series of payments crises began in the mid-1960s centering on the flow of funds into deutschemarks and out of sterling, dollars, and French francs. This was accentuated by rising rates of inflation in most countries as the postwar period progressed[35] and was later compounded by the oil price increases in the 1970s. Effective capital mobility in response to such balance-of-payments disequilibrium and consequent under- and over-valuation of exchange rates increased in large measure because of the relaxation of capital and exchange rate controls prevalent at the time of the Bretton Woods agreements. With the relaxation of controls as the postwar period progressed and the acceleration of changes in underlying economic and financial factors, there was a rapid expansion of capital movements during speculative crises through the 1960s and early 1970s (see table 1). The proximate cause of the breakdown of the adjustably pegged exchange rate system is well illustrated in these figures.

Given these important changes in underlying conditions, it is not at all inconsistent both to admire the Bretton Woods agreements as the foundation for the healthy development of the postwar international economy and to criticize the desirability of a par value system of exchange rate arrangements for the world as it has become in the 1960s and 1970s. Indeed, it can be argued that the changing world economy has necessitated a change in exchange rate procedures in order to continue to adhere to the basic principles of Bretton Woods.

---

[35] See Thomas D. Willett, "Secular Inflation and the International Monetary System," *Journal of Money, Credit and Banking*, vol. 5, no. 1, pt. 2 (1973), pp. 520–23.

Interest in Proposals for Greater Exchange Rate Flexibility

As the postwar period progressed, the disadvantages of the Bretton Woods par value exchange rate system became more apparent. Even prior to these developments, however, the conventional wisdom that the experiences of the interwar period had discredited floating rates had been challenged, most notably by Milton Friedman in his classic article in the early 1950s on flexible exchange rates.[36] As Friedman later noted, when this article was written, probably not more than 5 percent of the academic economists working in money and international trade would have supported substantially greater exchange rate flexibility.[37]

This strong academic consensus did not last for long. By the mid-1950s such prominent economists as Edward M. Bernstein, Gottfried Haberler, Friedrich Lutz, and James Meade, had written major pieces advocating substantially greater exchange rate flexibility.[38] By then it had become clear to researchers such as Haberler that dismantling widespread foreign exchange controls in Europe would not be feasible and sustainable unless greater exchange rate flexibility were adopted. Haberler's analysis proved to be correct. The restoration of general currency convertibility among the European countries did not come until the late 1950s and lasted only through the early and mid-1960s, when the defense of fixed parities began a retrogressive march toward wider use of controls.[39]

---

[36] Although Friedman's paper was written in the fall of 1950 for the Finance and Trade Division of the Office of Special Representative for Europe of the U.S. Economic Cooperation Administration, it did not receive public circulation until the publication of his book, *Essays in Positive Economics*, in 1953.

[37] Milton Friedman and Robert Roosa, *The Balance of Payments: Free Versus Fixed Exchange Rates* (Washington, D.C.: American Enterprise Institute, 1967), pp. 133–34.

[38] Edward M. Bernstein, "Strategic Factors in Balance of Payments Adjustment" I.M.F., *Staff Papers*, vol. 5, no. 2 (August 1956), pp. 151–69; Gottfried Haberler, *Currency Convertibility* (Washington, D.C.: American Enterprise Association, 1954); Lutz, *The Keynes and White Proposals*; and James E. Meade, "The Case for Variable Exchange Rates," *Three Banks Review*, no. 27 (September 1955), pp. 3–27.

[39] For discussions of the development of balance-of-payments policies during the postwar period, see, for example, Benjamin J. Cohen, *Balance of Payments Policies* (Middlesex, England: Penguin Books, 1969); Gottfried Haberler and Thomas D. Willett, *U.S. Balance of Payments Policies and International Monetary Reform* (Washington, D.C.: American Enterprise Institute, 1968); L. H. Officer and Thomas D. Willett, *The International Monetary System: Problems and Proposals* (Englewood Cliffs, N.J.: Prentice Hall, 1968), pt. 3; Susan Strange, *International Monetary Relations* (London: Oxford University Press, 1976); and Yeager, *International Monetary Relations*.

Table 1

THE SIZE OF SPECULATIVE CRISES

Date	Outflow from	Appreciating Currency	Known Reserve Movements
Oct. 20, 1960	U.S. dollar	gold	$300 million into Swiss francs in 4 days
March 10–13, 1961	sterling, U.S. dollar	D. mark, Sw. franc	$900 million of Canadian reserves lost January to June 25, 1962.
May–June 1962	Canadian dollar	D. mark, Sw. franc, guilder	
March 1964	lira		
Sept.–Nov. 24, 1964	sterling		
July–Sept. 10, 1965	sterling		
June, July 1966	sterling	Sw. franc	
May, June 1967	sterling[a]		$212 million into Swiss francs in first week of June 1967.
Nov., Dec. 1967	sterling, U.S. dollar	gold, D. mark, Sw. franc	$250 million lost by Bank of England on Friday, Nov. 17, 1967.
Jan., Feb. 1968	Canadian dollar		
March, 1968	sterling, U.S. dollar	gold	$400 million purchased by Bundesbank on Friday, March 15, 1968.

May, June 1968	sterling, Fr. franc		$1.5 billion official support to Fr. franc, March or June 1968.
Oct., Nov. 1968	sterling, Fr. franc	D. mark, Sw. franc	$850 million purchased by Bundesbank on November 18–19, 1968.
April, May 1969		D. mark	$2.5 billion purchased by Bundesbank in two days.
Sept., Oct. 1969		D. mark	$245 million purchased by Bundesbank in 1½ hours Sept. 29, 1969.
May, June 1970		Canadian dollar, D. mark	$640 million purchased by Bundesbank on June 10, 1970.
March, May 1971	U.S. dollar	D. mark, Sw. franc	$1 billion into European currencies in 40 minutes.
August 1971	U.S. dollar[b]		$3.7 billion into European currencies August 9–13, 1971.
June 1972	sterling		$2.6 billion lost by Bank of England, June 15–22, 1972.
Feb., March 1973	U.S. dollar[c]	yen, D. mark	$3 billion into European currencies on March 1, 1973.

[a] Sterling depreciated from $2.80 to $2.40 in November 1967.
[b] Dollar convertibility into gold suspended.
[c] Dollar devalued for second time, and then floated.

Source: Robert Russell, "Crisis Management in the International Monetary System, 1960–1973," paper presented at the March 1973 meeting of the International Studies Association in New York.

These developments were aptly described in 1965 by the Joint Economic Committee of the U.S. Congress in the following manner: "It is one of the many ironies and inconsistencies of modern life that, to protect fixed exchange rates—the means—we have compromised freedom of capital movements and to some extent, the ends which the fixed rates were intended to serve."[40]

By the mid-1960s Friedman could state that at least three-quarters of the relevant American academic community was in favor of greater flexibility of exchange rates.[41] The mounting difficulties in the operation of the adjustable peg system began to change some of the thinking in the business, financial and official communities. But official attention to possible reforms of the international monetary system during the 1960s focused primarily on questions of international liquidity. The issue of the exchange rate system was explicitly ruled out as a topic for the various official discussions of international monetary reform which began in the mid-1960s. Maintenance of the par value system had become an article of faith in official and "responsible" business and financial circles, and the par value system had itself become identified with the maintenance of fixed parities. Even the adjustable part of the adjustable peg system was considered taboo.

As Paul H. Douglas, the late senator and famous economist, described the official attitudes of that time:

> For years I have urged the Federal Reserve, the Treasury, and our representatives on the IMF to consider the flexible exchange rates, and I have been deeply disappointed by their refusal even to consider or study the matter. It has been an automatic reaction and, to tell the truth, I have not been able to generate any real argument. It has been a sort of tropismatic response, even below the level of instinct.[42]

By the mid and late 1960s, however, a broader range of people outside the academic community began to realize that discussions of international monetary reforms could no longer be limited to issues of international liquidity. This environment encouraged economists to develop and advocate proposals for greater flexibility into the exchange rate system.[43] With wider recognition that the Bretton

---

[40] Joint Economic Committee, *Guidelines for Improving the International Monetary System*, 89th Congress, 2d session, 1966, p. 18.

[41] Friedman and Roosa, *The Balance of Payments*, p. 1933.

[42] Paul H. Douglas, *America in the Market Place* (New York: Holt, Rinehart and Winston, 1966), p. 576.

[43] Some of the most notable papers advocating various forms of greater, but limited, exchange rate flexibility in the mid-1960s include: J. Black, "A Proposal

Woods system was not one of genuinely fixed exchange rates, "practical" people became interested in the argument that more frequent and consequently smaller changes in exchange rates might be less disruptive than infrequent and large changes in exchange rates, which in the interim had to be maintained by various types of capital and exchange controls and were buffeted by repeated crises. Proposals for wider bands around parities and for crawling pegs or sliding parities were attractive because they could allow more frequent, smoother exchange rate adjustments without abandoning the concept of exchange rate parities.

The idea of crawling pegs or sliding parities was technically superior to the adjustably pegged exchange rate system adopted at Bretton Woods as a way of providing exchange rate fixity in the short run and exchange rate flexibility in the long run.[44] In my judgment wider bands were shown to be of only limited usefulness by themselves in improving the operation of an adjustably pegged rate system, but as an adjunct to the adoption of crawling pegs, they could reduce problems of speculative capital flows.[45]

---

for the Reform of Exchange Rates," *Economic Journal*, vol. 76, no. 302 (June 1966), pp. 288–95; William Fellner, "On Limited Exchange Rate Flexibility," in Fellner et al., eds., *Maintaining and Restoring Balance in International Payments* (Princeton: Princeton University Press, 1966), pp. 111–22; R. M. Goodwin, "Stabilizing the Exchange Rate," *Review of Economics and Statistics*, vol. 46, no. 2 (May 1964), pp. 160–62; Halm, *The "Band" Proposal*; Fritz Machlup, *Plans for Reform of the International Monetary System*, Princeton Special Paper on International Finance, no. 3 (August 1962), rev. ed., March 1964; James E. Meade, "The International Monetary Mechanism," *Three Banks Review*, no. 64 (September 1964), pp. 3–25, and "Exchange Rate Flexibility," *International Payments Problems* (Washington, D.C.: American Enterprise Institute, 1966), pp. 71–80; J. Carter Murphy, "Moderated Exchange-Rate Variability: Reply," *National Banking Review*, vol. 4, no. 1 (September 1966), pp. 101–105; and John H. Williamson, *The Crawling Peg*, Princeton Essays in International Finance, no. 50 (December 1965). Extensive discussion and several more proposals appear in George Halm, ed., *Approaches to Greater Flexibility of Exchange Rates: The Bürgenstock Papers* (Princeton: Princeton University Press, 1970).

[44] In this regard, Katz presents the most able defense of the par value system that I have seen. He loads his presentation inappropriately, however, in favor of the par value system by treating it as the only form of managed exchange rate flexibility to be compared with the extremes of freely floating and genuinely fixed rates. Katz argues convincingly that many countries would prefer managed flexibility on domestic stabilization grounds, but does not really address the question of whether an adjustable peg is an effective form of managed flexibility. In this respect, the adjustable peg system is probably the least desirable of all major versions of managed floating. Samuel I. Katz, *The Case for the Par-Value System*, Princeton Essays in International Finance, no. 92 (March 1972). See, for example, Thomas D. Willett, "The Eurocurrency Market, Exchange Rate Systems, and National Financial Policy," Carl Stem, Dennis Logue, and John Makin, eds., *Eurocurrencies and the International Monetary System* (Washington, D.C.: American Enterprise Institute, 1976).

[45] Not all advocates of crawling pegs, however, also advocated substantially

19

The most serious technical objection raised against the replacement of adjustable pegs with sliding parities was that this might cause speculative capital flows and place a strong constraint on domestic monetary policies. This was frequently referred to as the problem of the interest rate constraint under crawling pegs. Further analysis, however, suggested that while a system of sliding parities could certainly give rise to difficulties on this score, there was a strong presumption that these difficulties would be less severe than under the adjustable peg.[46]

An important qualification should be noted, however. Although this conclusion was valid for genuine systems of crawling pegs, it did not necessarily carry over to the idea, frequently expressed during this period, of borrowing a little from the crawling peg system and making adjustments in parities more frequently than had occurred in practice under the Bretton Woods system, say every year or two. Sometimes called the "new-look" Bretton Woods approach, it would probably have proved to be the worst possible type of system in terms of generating speculative capital flows, as was particularly emphasized by Gottfried Haberler.[47]

The vast amount of intellectual and negotiating efforts that went into the discussions on improving the par value system had little direct influence on actual exchange rate practices. The very developments which were making "practical" people finally realize that the adjustable peg system was unsatisfactory were likewise undermining the potential workability of the proposals for limited exchange rate flexibility. As was noted by leading advocates such as Ronald McKinnon, the case for crawling pegs depended on a fairly high degree

---

wider bands. See, for example, Ronald McKinnon, "Exchange-Rate Flexibility and Monetary Policy," *Journal of Money, Credit and Banking*, vol. 3, no. 2 (May 1971), pp. 339–55.

[46] See Thomas D. Willett, "Short-term Capital Movements and the Interest Rate Constraint Under Systems of Limited Flexibility of Exchange Rates," Halm, *Approaches to Greater Flexibility*, pp. 283–94; and Thomas D. Willett, Samuel I. Katz, and William H. Branson, *Exchange Rate Systems, Interest Rates, and Capital Flows*, Princeton Essays in International Finance, no. 78 (January 1970). One issue that was never fully resolved in the discussion of this topic was whether on balance under a crawling peg the possibility of discreet adjustments in parities should be completely ruled out. A number of advocates of crawling pegs argued that they should be ruled out; but when large disequilibriums emerge rapidly, the crawling peg is not a very efficient method of adjustment. On balance, my hunch is that it would not have been desirable to attempt to "outlaw" discreet parity adjustment under a crawling peg, but there was far from a consensus on the issue.

[47] See, for example, Haberler's foreword to Juergen B. Donges, *Brazil's Trotting Peg* (Washington, D.C.: American Enterprise Institute, 1971), pp. 4–5, and Gottfried Haberler, *The World Economy*, p. 37.

of underlying economic stability in the world economy.[48] However, by the time crawling pegs came under serious official consideration, world inflation had accelerated to the point that the necessary conditions for a well-functioning system of crawling pegs were no longer met.

Any doubts on this score were removed by the instabilities generated by the oil price increases in 1973 and 1974. As I have argued elsewhere, it seems quite possible that when conditions in the international economy are fairly stable to begin with, then a system of crawling pegs might be able to generate still more stability, but when such underlying stability in the world economy is absent, then attempts to maintain a system of sliding parities would generate even greater instability.[49] Sliding parities might have been an excellent system for the 1950s, but not for the 1970s.

In the end this intermediate stage of crawling pegs was almost entirely skipped as the world moved to the widespread use of floating rates, albeit in many instances, heavily managed. Although the discussion and negotiations on mechanisms for greater exchange rate flexibility did not weigh nearly as heavily as events in generating the reform of the exchange rate system, their contribution in influencing the attitudes of government officials and international bankers and businessmen toward flexible exchange rates was not negligible.

Opposition to floating rates did not die quickly, however. Those who had confused the basic principles of Bretton Woods with its procedures, viewed fixed exchange rates as the symbol of international financial cooperation. Criticisms were seen as attacks on the very concept of a well-ordered international monetary system.[50]

Despite mounting evidence in the 1960s that there were serious deficiencies in the operation of the international adjustment process, official reports continued to give serious consideration only to marginal changes in the exchange rate system, such as somewhat wider bands and prompter use of par value adjustments.[51] A cold shoulder

---

[48] See, for example, McKinnon, "Exchange Rate Flexibility," p. 354.

[49] Willett, "The Eurocurrency Market."

[50] See, for example, Willett, "Our Evolving International Economic System."

[51] See, for example, *The Role of Exchange Rates in the Adjustment of International Payments*, Report by the Executive Directors of the International Monetary Fund, Washington, D.C., 1970, and *Reform of the International Monetary System*, Report by the Executive Directors of the International Monetary Fund, Washington, D.C., 1972. An excellent critique of the first report is given in Halm, *International Monetary Fund and Flexibility*. Alternate Executive Director of the IMF Tom de Vries has written that this report "came down squarely on the side of maintenance even strengthening of the Bretton Woods par value system, and only in the most tentative way discussed such frightening matters as a 'slight widening in the margins around parity.' " In this, the Executive Board

was given to the many proposals made during the late 1960s and early 1970s for substantially greater, but still limited, exchange rate flexibility through the adoption of so-called sliding parities or crawling pegs.

The Initiation of Widespread Floating and the Process of International Monetary Reform

Such official attitudes, however, could not turn back the clock and recreate the conditions under which a par value system would be workable. Given the evolution of the world economy, widespread adoption of floating exchange rates was probably inevitable. When it came, temporarily during 1971 and then again in 1973, it was as a crisis response to unsustainable disequilibrium in the foreign exchange markets and not as the result of a planned international monetary reform.

Even after the second initiation of widespread exchange rate flexibility in 1973, the announced objective of official reform negotiations was to secure a prompt return to a system of "stable but adjustable" par values, although with allowance for floating rates in particular circumstances.[52] The negotiations on international monetary reform by the Committee of Twenty (C-20) during the period 1972–1974 must be considered in this light. Negotiators gradually discovered that living with floating exchange rates was not as terrible as they had feared. Indeed, as is reviewed in chapter 2, our recent experience with floating, while by no means ideal, has come much closer to the expectations of the supporters than of the critics of floating rates. As negotiations progressed, this experience was combined with increased recognition of the difficulties in reestablishing a workable par value system, even one based on wider margins and prompter parity adjustments. By the beginning of 1974, most of the negotiators realized that an early return to a par value system was

faithfully reflected the prevailing opinion in official circles. Only in the United States, Germany, and Canada had doubts about the par value system begun to stir. Tom de Vries, "Jamaica or the Non-Reform of the International Monetary System," *Foreign Affairs*, vol. 54, no. 3 (April 1976), p. 581.

[52] The communique issued by the Committee of Twenty (the official negotiating body) after its meeting of March 26–27, 1973, shortly after the breakdown of the Smithsonian realignment of pegged exchange rates, reads in part, ". . . in the reformed system the exchange rate regime should remain based on stable but adjustable par values. It was also recognized that floating rates could provide a useful technique in particular circumstances." As Tom de Vries notes, however, "it had been pointed out at the meeting itself that 'particular' did not mean 'temporary' and was not equivalent to 'short-term' " ("Jamaica," p. 586).

neither feasible nor urgently needed, and some indeed began to doubt whether such a restoration would be desirable even if it were feasible.

Negotiations began to develop along a two-track system—one track focusing on improvement of international financial cooperation under floating exchange rates, and the other continuing to focus on what a new par value system might look like in the future. This two-track system culminated in publication by the IMF of the *Outline of Reform*[53] which discussed some short-term measures such as guidelines for floating exchange rates as well as alternatives for longer term reform based on a return to a system of "stable but adjustable par values."

In many official quarters, reluctance to acknowledge the long-term viability of a system of flexible exchange rates died hard. Official explanations of the postponement of attempts to restore a par value system frequently focused on the uncertainties generated by the huge oil price increases in 1973 and 1974. Even in the absence of the oil shocks, however, it was widely recognized that restoration of a par value system in the short or even medium term was not really a viable option. It was, however, almost another two years before the reform exercise was finally completed at Jamaica in early 1976, and the system of floating exchange rates was officially sanctioned.[54]

Basic agreement on the nature of the monetary reform was achieved among the major industrial countries at the meetings of the heads of state at Rambouillet, France, in November 1975. These proposals were refined at the December meeting of the G-10 in Paris, and agreement on the full reform package was secured at the meeting of the Interim Committee of the Governors of the International Monetary Fund at Kingston, Jamaica, on January 7–8, 1976.[55]

---

[53] *Outline of Reform with Accompanying Annexes* in IMF, *Survey Outline of Reform Supplement* (Washington, D.C.: International Monetary Fund, June 17, 1974).

[54] The formal process of amending the Articles of Agreement of the International Monetary Fund is not yet completed, as in many countries, such as the United States, enabling legislation is required. The new articles will become the Second Amendment. Throughout this study, these are referred to as the Jamaica Agreements or Jamaica Reforms, but these reforms are also frequently referred to as the Second Amendment.

[55] In addition to the matters of balance-of-payments adjustment and flexible exchange rates, the Jamaica Agreements also dealt with the role of gold and SDR, and the resources and operations of the IMF. The participants agreed to diminish the role of gold in the system (1) by abolishing its official price, which had been used to express the value of currencies, SDRs, and Fund obligations, (2) by eliminating gold from transactions with the Fund, and (3) by empowering the Fund to dispose of its gold holdings and place the profits from the resultant auctions in a new trust fund to be used for assisting low-income developing

Given the strong official support for fixed rates it is perhaps not surprising that the negotiating process took so long. Where conflicts with previous positions and associated prestige are at stake, officials have often demonstrated a willingness to accept changes in practice long before they have been willing to accept them formally. And indeed international legalization of floating was made possible by a compromise requiring that the new amendments discuss at length mechanisms by which a par value, pegged rate system could be restored, thus allowing past advocates of pegging to claim a measure of diplomatic victory.[56]

To many the Jamaica Agreements were anticlimatic because they represented the codification and legalization of the monetary system that had already evolved, rather than the creation of some brave new structure. But there is an unwritten general rule in international monetary relations that the less dramatic the international monetary developments, the better the system is working. The Jamaica Agreements are no exception to this rule.

The full significance of this reform in our international exchange rate system is still not fully recognized even by many international financial experts. It is argued in chapter 3 that many of the criticisms of the Jamaica Agreements are due to failure to appreciate how fundamental a change has been brought about by the adoption of floating exchange rates. Undoubtedly one of the main reasons for charges that the Jamaica Agreements represent only partial reform is that they do not contain a large portion of the proposals for long-term reform presented in the Committee of Twenty's 1974 *Outline of Reform*, which assumed restoration of a stable but adjustable par value exchange rate system. There is little question that the Jamaica Agreements would be woefully inadequate for this purpose.

---

countries with severe balance-of-payments problems. Furthermore, a series of technical decisions were taken to facilitate and broaden the use of SDR in the hope that the withdrawal of gold would be accompanied by an enhanced role for the SDR as a reserve asset and unit of account. The participants also agreed to increase overall IMF quotas by 33.6 percent—doubling oil-exporting country shares and reducing the developed member shares—and provided that future passage of major Fund decisions would depend upon 85 percent rather than 80 percent of the vote. Finally, a series of operational changes were made in the IMF Articles of Agreement to grant the Fund more authority over the lending, investment, and repurchase of its usable resources.

[56] A similar negotiating compromise facilitated agreement on the First Amendment to the IMF Articles, creating the new international reserve SDRs in 1969. One of the major issues of debate had been whether a new reserve asset should be created or whether IMF credit facilities should be expanded. By naming the new creation Special Drawing Rights and endowing it with some credit-like features, a new reserve asset was created, while still allowing the opponents to claim some degree of victory.

Despite the disporportionate amount of legal language in the agreements devoted to the possibilities of reestablishing a par value system, in substance the Jamaica Agreements reflect acceptance of floating exchange rates as the basis for our international monetary system for the indefinite future. While reaffirming the importance of international cooperation and exchange rate stability, they recognize that such exchange rate stability can only be achieved as the result of the restoration of stability in underlying economic and financial conditions. Exchange rate stability of any lasting duration cannot be imposed externally by adoption of the pegged exchange rates and heavy official intervention in the foreign exchange market.

Acceptance of floating rates has led to substantial improvements in the operation of the international monetary system with respect to all three of the major problems of any international monetary system—liquidity, confidence, and adjustment. Given the difficulties in reaching agreement on monetary reform among more than 100 countries, this is no small achievement.

Of course, the Jamaica Agreements do not solve all international monetary problems; no reform could do that. But they do present a strong framework for dealing with international monetary problems as they evolve. Thus, despite the failure to adopt many of the pet schemes (including some of my own) for solving this or that issue put forth by international monetary experts, by realistic standards the Jamaica Agreements must be judged a comprehensive rather than partial revision of the international monetary system established at Bretton Woods. In the following chapters the performance of floating rates and the major aspects of our new international monetary system will be analyzed in more detail.

2
THE PERFORMANCE OF FLOATING RATES

Overview and Summary

By the time widespread floating of exchange rates was initiated in the 1970s there had been a substantial swing in the views of academic economists toward favoring floating. A more receptive attitude was emerging in banking, business, and official circles. Still, however, there were many academic critics and a majority of international monetary officials who initially continued to oppose floating as anything but a short-term emergency measure. Not surprisingly, initial evaluations of how floating was working tended to correlate highly with positions taken before the initiation of floating. "Objective" evaluations were made particularly difficult by the high degree of underlying economic and financial instability which had contributed to the breakdown of the par value system, and the foreign exchange markets were still in the process of transitional adjustment to the new system when the world was hit by the huge increases in oil prices in late 1973 and early 1974. Thus critics could point to many examples of chaotic conditions and behavior in the foreign exchange markets, while supporters of floating could argue that these were primarily the results of transitional adjustments and the instability of underlying economic and financial conditions.

It is still not possible to draw definitive conclusions on many aspects of the performance of floating rates, but it has become increasingly clear that while not all of the hopes of advocates of floating have been fulfilled, still less have the major fears of the critics been realized. For example, there was not the breakdown of international financial cooperation and reversion to the nationalist economic warfare of the 1930s, which many critics had predicted would accompany generalized floating. And this was true despite the additional pressures generated by the oil crisis. Nor have the critics' predictions of a substantial crippling of world trade proven correct. And while there are still disagreements about technical aspects of the efficiency of operation of speculation and the exchange markets, there has been a noticeably high correlation between the stability of underlying conditions and the stability in the exchange markets. For example, the series of cycles in the dollar–German mark exchange rate during 1973 and 1974 (see figure 1) prompted many allegations of bandwagons and other types of poorly behaved speculation in the early days of the float. But as underlying conditions have stabilized, so has the dollar-mark exchange rate. Private speculation has certainly not worked perfectly, but neither has it undermined the operation of floating rates as many writers in earlier periods would have expected.

There are still many open questions with respect to optimal intervention policies under floating rates, but there can be little remaining question that managed floating is a highly viable system. While it is easy to point ex post to episodes in which more official intervention might have been desirable and to ones in which less intervention probably would have been preferable, there is little question in my mind that to date the system of managed floating, imperfect as it has been, has performed much better than would have a general par value system. Thus I strongly concur with Edward Bernstein's judgment that,

> As a practical matter the system of fluctuating exchange rates has worked reasonably well, much better than would have been possible if attempts had been made to perpetuate the Bretton Woods system of fixed parities by patchwork here and there.[1]

Indeed this is now a majority view and is reflected in the Rambouillet and Jamaica agreements.

Opposition to floating rates has not been totally quelled, however.[2] Officials frequently find it convenient to blame their domestic economic difficulties at least in part on the operation of the international monetary system, and floating rates have not been exempted from such attacks. Likewise there are still some academic critics who

---

[1] Edward M. Bernstein, "Monetary Authorities and the Free Exchange Market," speech to Foreign Exchange Conference of American Bankers Association, New York, November 4, 1976.

[2] See, for example, Paul Lewis, "The Weak Get Weaker With Floating Rates," *New York Times*, October 10, 1976, and Edward Dale, "Industrialized Bloc Finds Problems in Floating Rates of Exchange," *New York Times*, October 6, 1976.

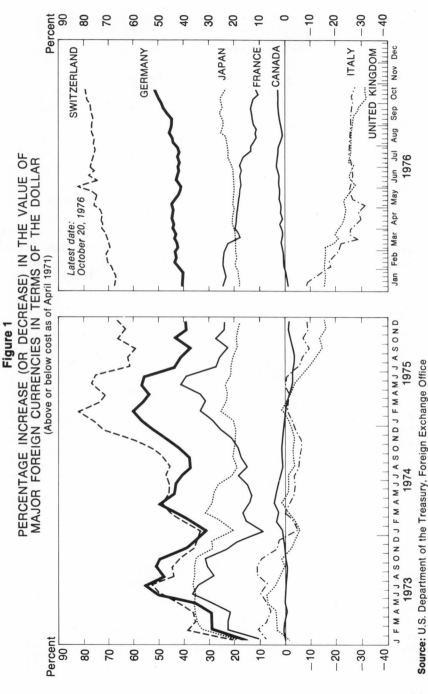

Figure 1

PERCENTAGE INCREASE (OR DECREASE) IN THE VALUE OF
MAJOR FOREIGN CURRENCIES IN TERMS OF THE DOLLAR

(Above or below cost as of April 1971)

Percent

90
80
70
60
50
40
30
20
10
0
−10
−20
−30
−40

SWITZERLAND

GERMANY

JAPAN

FRANCE

CANADA

ITALY

UNITED KINGDOM

Latest date:
October 20, 1976

Percent

90
80
70
60
50
40
30
20
10
0
−10
−20
−30
−40

J F M A M J J A S O N D J F M A M J J A S O N D J F M A M J J A S O N D
1973   1974   1975

Jan Feb Mar Apr May Jun Jul Aug Sep Oct Nov Dec
1976

Source: U.S. Department of the Treasury, Foreign Exchange Office

29

argue that floating rates really do not work and that they are a major cause of world inflation.

Some critics also object that the current system is not one of freely floating exchange rates for all countries. Official intervention in foreign exchange markets certainly has not ceased; to the contrary, over a number of intervals under the current float, intervention has been higher than during the same length periods under the par value system.[3] Even with official management, only a minority of the over 100 countries in the world are floating their currencies independently. These are, however, primarily the larger industrial countries, which, despite their small number, account for a substantial portion of world trade.[4]

But serious proponents of floating neither anticipated nor advocated that all countries should adopt floating rates. Milton Friedman, for example, was careful in his 1950 article on floating rates to indicate that a general system of floating rates did not mean that every country should float independently.[5] The literature on the theory of optimum currency areas explores the many factors affecting the desirability of floating independently versus joining with one or more other countries to form a currency area.[6] Advocacy of generalized

---

[3] This combination of both greater reserve use and greater flexibility of exchange rates does not disprove the standard economic argument that the need for reserves is less with greater exchange rate flexibility. During this period, there were also greater disturbances; so that while both intervention and exchange rate movements increased, there is a strong presumption that in the absence of greater exchange rate flexibility, reserve flows would have been still greater. As Sir Roy Harrod and John Williamson have shown, it is theoretically possible for there to be circumstances in which a move to managed floating would actually increase intervention, but as Black has noted, this seems likely to be primarily a theoretical *curiosum* with little practical relevance. For recent discussions on this issue, see John Williamson, "Exchange Rate Flexibility and Reserve Use," and Stanley W. Black's comment in *The Scandinavian Journal of Economics*, vol. 78, no. 2 (1976), pp. 327–34 and 340–45, respectively; Gottfried Haberler, "How Important is Control Over International Reserves?" (Paper presented at the Marcus Fleming Memorial Conference on the New International Monetary System, International Monetary Fund, November 11–12, 1976); and Esther C. Suss, "A Note on Reserve Use Under Alternative Exchange Rate Regimes," IMF, *Staff Papers*, vol. 23, no. 2 (July 1976), pp. 387–94.

[4] For example, the International Monetary Fund's *Annual Report, 1975* classified only 11 of 122 currencies as floating independently as of June 30, 1975, with another seven as members of a joint float; but these countries accounted for 46.4 and 23.2 percent of the international trade by IMF members (table 9, p. 24). The difficulties of attempting to classify various types of exchange rate regimes are further discussed in the *Annual Report, 1976*, pp. 24–25.

[5] Friedman, "The Case for Flexible Exchange Rates."

[6] For a review of this literature, see Edward Tower and Thomas D. Willett, *The Theory of Optimum Currency Areas and Exchange-Rate Flexibility* (Princeton, N.J.: Princeton International Finance Section, Special Papers in International Finance, no. 11, May 1976). A good bit of interesting empirical work is now

flexibility by most economists is based on the belief that the international system should allow countries to adopt flexible exchange rates without sanction or stigma, not that all countries should be forced to float.

The following sections analyze the major criticisms which have been raised against floating.[7] There are many reasons why countries may not wish to abstain completely from intervention in their foreign exchange markets. But arguments for a managed instead of a free float are not the same as arguments for a return to a generalized par value system. National management of exchange rates makes desirable continuing international surveillance of the adjustment process under floating. But this can hardly be considered a black mark against floating in general, as some critics have implied. And for the arguments that do call for a return to generally pegged exchange rates, little support is found. The adoption of floating rates clearly has not solved all of the problems of the international monetary system, but man-

---

going on in this area. See, for example, Jacob Dreyer, "Determinants of Exchange-Rate Regimes for Currencies of Developing Countries" (Paper presented at the annual meetings of the Allied Social Science Association, Atlantic City, New Jersey, September 16–18, 1976); R. Robert Heller, "Exchange-Rate Flexibility and Currency Areas" (Paper presented at the Fourth Paris-Dauphine Conference on Money and International Monetary Problems, November 1–3, 1976); and Paul Holden, "The Demand for International Reserves and the Choice of Exchange Rate Regime: An Empirical Analysis" (Ph.D. diss., Duke University, 1976).

[7] The discussion in this chapter draws primarily on the experiences of the industrial countries under the current float. Some representatives from the developing countries have been particularly vocal in charging, especially during the earlier days of the float, that their countries were especially hurt by the adoption of generalized floating. While floating did undoubtedly present some new complications for the developing countries in terms of intervention policy and the choice of what major currency, if any, to peg to, the charges against floating of the less developed countries, or LDCs, tended to be greatly exaggerated and were often implicitly based on unrealistic comparisons with an ideal situation of genuinely fixed rates, fully coordinated monetary policies, and no controls. In reality, the LDCs were indirectly one of the greatest victims of the poor operation of the adjustable peg system. See, for example, Officer and Willett, *The International Monetary System*, pp. 229–30. Thus, they stood to have much to gain from the operation of a well-functioning system of floating rates. For discussions of the effects of alternative exchange rate systems on the developing countries, see Stanley W. Black, "Exchange Rate Policies for Less Developed Countries in a World of Floating Rates" (University of Stockholm, Institute for International Economic Studies, Seminar Paper no. 53); J. H. Bhagwati, "International Monetary System," *Journal of International Economics*, vol. 2, no. 4 (September 1972), pp. 321–22; William Cline, *Flexible Exchange Rates and the Developing Countries* (Washington, D.C.: The Brookings Institution, 1975); Carlos Díaz Alejandro, *Less Developed Countries and the Post-1971 International Financial System*, Princeton Essays in International Finance, no. 94 (July 1972); and Thomas D. Willett and Nicholas P. Sargen, "Exchange-Rate Flexibility, Objective Indicators, and International Monetary Reform," sections 6 and 7, in Patrick M. Boarman and David B. Tuerck, eds., *World Monetary Disorder* (New York: Praeger, 1976).

aged flexibility does provide the soundest foundation for the future evolution of the system.

Speculation and Exchange Rate Volatility

One of the most frequent criticisms of the performance of floating exchange rates is the charge that they have been excessively volatile because of destabilizing or insufficient stabilizing speculation.[8] In addition to the volatility of rates as an indication of poor performance of floating rates, critics have pointed to the increase of transactions costs and the worsening of the accuracy of forward rates as predictors of future spot rates. Despite the frequency of such charges, however, little systematic evidence has in fact been offered that the foreign exchange markets have been dominated by badly behaved speculative forces. As was noted above, volatility in exchange markets can also be explained in terms of the instability of the underlying international economic environment. The same holds for higher transactions costs and the poorer prediction record of forward rates.

---

[8] See, for example, Charles P. Kindleberger, "Lessons of Floating Exchange Rates," Carnegie-Rochester Conference Series on Public Policy, vol. 3, *Journal of Monetary Economics* (1976), pp. 51–76, and Ronald I. McKinnon, "Floating Exchange Rates, 1973–1974: The Emperor's New Clothes," Carnegie-Rochester Conference Series on Public Policy, vol. 3, *Journal of Monetary Economics* (1976), pp. 79–114. In this study, stabilizing speculation refers to speculation that moves the exchange rate toward its equilibrium value, and destabilizing speculation is speculation that moves the rate away from its equilibrium value. Of course, equilibrium is an ambiguous theoretical concept, and not all reasonable people are likely to concur on what exchange rate corresponds to any particular concept of equilibrium. But defining stabilizing and destabilizing in this way does force discussions to focus on the correct issues, even if operational answers cannot always be agreed upon. Following this terminology, insufficiently stabilizing speculation refers to speculation that moves the current market rate toward its equilibrium level, but is not sufficiently strong to move it fully to the equilibrium level. In practice, the term generally means instances in which the movement toward equilibrium fell substantially short. For convenience I shall use the terms *poorly behaved* or *badly behaved* speculation to refer to speculation that is either actively destabilizing or insufficiently stabilizing. For further discussion of the concepts of stabilizing and destabilizing speculation and efficiency in foreign exchange markets, and the inappropriateness of taking exchange rate variability per se as an indication of poorly behaved speculation, see Steven W. Kohlhagen, "The Foreign Exchange Markets—Models, Tests and Empirical Evidence," (Paper presented at the Treasury Workshop on Technical Studies on Exchange Rate Flexibility, February 1976); Kohlhagen, "The Identification of Destabilizing Foreign Exchange Speculation," Federal Reserve Board International Finance Discussion Paper no. 100 (January 1977); and Richard J. Sweeney and Thomas D. Willett, "Concepts of Efficiency and Speculation in the Foreign Exchange Market," in Richard J. Sweeney and Thomas D. Willett, eds., *Exchange Rate Flexibility and International Monetary Stability* (Washington, D.C.: American Enterprise Institute, forthcoming).

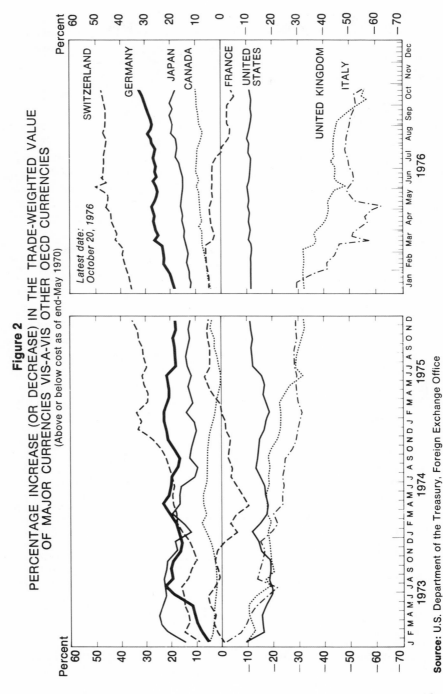

Figure 2

PERCENTAGE INCREASE (OR DECREASE) IN THE TRADE-WEIGHTED VALUE
OF MAJOR CURRENCIES VIS-A-VIS OTHER OECD CURRENCIES
(Above or below cost as of end-May 1970)

Source: U.S. Department of the Treasury, Foreign Exchange Office

33

It should also be noted that, as is indicated in figures 1 and 2, trade weighted indexes of exchange rates have generally shown considerably less fluctuation than have the bilateral exchange rates between the dollar and such currencies as the German mark and Swiss franc which have been pointed to so frequently by critics.[9]

Care must also be taken in judging the appropriateness of exchange rate fluctuations. It is not legitimate to assume, as many critics have, that any large rapid movement in exchange rates is necessarily due to perverse speculative forces. Some apparently believe that the fundamental factors which determine equilibrium exchange rates can change only slowly. Thus they argue, large rapid changes in exchange rates cannot be "appropriate." There is increased recognition today that exchange rate changes may be necessary to maintain equilibrium, but there has been a disturbing tendency for many commentators to adopt the benchmark that exchange rate changes should reflect only relative inflation rates. One frequently encounters judgments about the appropriateness of exchange rates based on the results of simple calculations of relative national price movements. Implicitly such views assume that only trade competitiveness "should" influence exchange rates and that trade competitiveness can be sufficiently closely approximated by relative movements in particular sets of price statistics to be used for exchange rate policy. But neither of these propositions is soundly based. Trade flows can hardly be considered the only component of the balance of payments which should appropriately influence exchange rates, nor can the many factors influencing competitiveness be captured adequately in a single set of price calculations.[10]

---

[9] There is no easy answer to the question of what type of measure "should" be used. The answers vary from one type of question to another. For example, one type of measure may be best for investigating effects on inflation, and another for investigating effects on risk and uncertainties. Likewise for considering the effects on risk and uncertainties, the appropriate measure of currency variability will vary with the particular transactor. For firms that deal with only a single foreign country, fluctuations in the bilateral rate of exchange are clearly most relevant. For enterprises that are more diversified, the behavior of composite measures of exchange rate movements would also have to be considered. Insofar as exchange rate changes vis à vis a particular currency tend to be offsetting, the variability of individual bilateral rates will overstate the degree of variability of the composite. On the issues of what types of exchange rate measures are most appropriately used for different purposes, see David Klock, Charles Pigott, and Thomas D. Willett, "The Use of Composite Exchange Rate Indicators" and Charles Pigott, Richard Sweeney, and Thomas D. Willett, "The Resource Allocation Effects of Exchange Rate Variations," both in Sweeney and Willett, eds., *Exchange-Rate Flexibility.*

[10] For further discussion of these points, see Charles Pigott, John Rutledge, Richard J. Sweeney, and Thomas D. Willett, "Alternative Approaches to Ex-

Furthermore, the appropriateness of exchange rate developments cannot be judged exclusively on the basis of *ex post* developments in underlying factors. Expectations of the effects of both current and future developments in underlying economic factors do and should influence current exchange rates. Once this is realized it becomes easier to understand that large rapid movements of exchange rates are not necessarily evidence of badly behaved speculation.

Consider, for example, the sizable changes in "equilibrium" exchange rates that might be associated with substantially altered patterns of OPEC capital flows. Expectations about such flows may quite rationally shift by sizable amounts from time to time and corresponding shifts in expectations about the levels of equilibrium exchange rates may be considerable.[11] But, if some of these shifts are later reversed, this is not necessarily an indication that exchange rate adjustments should not have occurred. Only if the reversal was predictable should it not have influenced the exchange rate. In an efficient speculative market, prices reflect best guesses about future developments and attempts artificially to suppress price movements run the risk of distorting allocative signals. *Ceteris paribus*, less variability in exchange rates is to be preferred to more, but it is only in instances in which private speculation is performing inefficiently that attempts to reduce variability in exchange rates directly would be efficient. As was recognized in the Rambouillet and Jamaica agreements, except in instances in which speculation is behaving poorly, the only way genuinely to enhance the stability of exchange rates is to reduce the instability of underlying economic and financial conditions.

Thus, neither animal spirits nor the gnomes of Zurich are required to explain why there has been a good deal of exchange rate volatility under the current float. There can be little question, for example, that a not insignificant part of the fluctuations in the dollar—deutsche mark exchange rate during 1973 and 1974 can be explained in terms of reasonable speculative responses to expectations of the effects of the oil crisis and OPEC capital flows.

Particular episodes of large rapid exchange rate movements can also be explained in terms of the effects of destabilizing official intervention policies. For example, in more than one instance prolonged official resistance to exchange rate movements allowed a substantial

---

change Market Intervention," in Sweeney and Willett, eds., *Exchange-Rate Flexibility*.

[11] See Thomas D. Willett, "Analyzing the Causes of Exchange Rate Changes," and Dean De Rosa, "Simulations of the Exchange Rate Effects of Changes in Expected Equilibrium Current Account Positions," both in Sweeney and Willett, eds., *Exchange-Rate Flexibility*.

disequilibrium to develop and when the need to let the rate go was finally recognized, it is not surprising that large rapid movements in the rate frequently resulted.

It must be acknowledged, however, that establishing that large exchange rate fluctuations are not necessarily the result of speculative inefficiencies is not the same as establishing that speculation has always behaved desirably and that all observed fluctuations in exchange rates can be explained in benign terms. Indeed, few of even the strongest advocates of floating would expect the latter to be true. Nor can we expect to be able to achieve complete agreement on all the instances in which speculation was well or poorly behaved, for this would require knowledge of both speculators' expectations of underlying developments and knowledge of the "true" econometric model of the foreign exchange market.

This does not, however, mean that we cannot reasonably expect to gain substantive knowledge about speculative behavior through systematic empirical investigations. Some of the major popular theories about speculation do imply testable hypotheses about the behavior of exchange rates. For example, the finding of sizable systematic cycles or patterns in exchange rates would be consistent with the prevalence of poorly behaved speculation, either actively destabilizing bandwagon effects or at least an absence of sufficient stabilizing speculation to eliminate the profit potential inherent in such patterns.[12]

By the use of techniques such as filter rules it is possible to test for the persistence of patterns which are indicative of speculative inefficiency.[13] Such testing has frequently been misunderstood as be-

---

[12] A number of writers have suggested that the latter may frequently be the case. See, for example, "The Drift Back to Fixed Exchange Rates," *Business Week* (June 2, 1975), pp. 60–63; James Burtle, "Some Problems in Living With a System of Floating Exchange Rates," *Business Economics*, vol. 9, no. 2 (May 1974); Fred Hirsch and David Hinham, "Floating Rates—Expectations and Experience," *Three Banks Review*, no. 102 (June 1974), pp. 3–34; Ronald McKinnon's review of *The Alignment of Foreign Exchange Rates*, by Fritz Machlup, *Journal of International Economics*, vol. 5, no. 1 (February 1975), pp. 99–101; and Marina Whitman, "The Payments Adjustment Process and the Exchange Rate Regime, What Have We Learned?," *The American Economic Review: Papers and Proceedings*, vol. 65, no. 2 (May 1975), pp. 133–46.

[13] See, for example, Michael P. Dooley and Jeffrey R. Shafer, "Analysis of Short-Run Exchange Rate Behavior: March, 1973 to September, 1975" Federal Reserve Board International Finance Discussion Paper no. 76 (February 1976); Ian Giddy and Gunter Dufey, "The Random Behavior of Flexible Exchange Rates: Implications for Forecasting," *Journal of International Business Studies*, vol. 6, no. 1 (Spring 1975), pp. 1–32; Dennis Logue, Richard J. Sweeney, and Thomas D. Willett, "The Speculative Behavior of Foreign Exchange Rates During the Current Float," *Journal of Business Research*, forthcoming, and "Statistical Testing of the Speculative Behavior of Foreign Exchange Rates," in Sweeney and Willett,

ing rather esoteric and concerned only with a particular rather technical aspect of exchange market performance. In fact, however, it is directly relevant to the basic issue of the effects of floating exchange rates on economic efficiency, does speculation behave poorly or not. Admittedly the results of such testing can be only one-sided. The existence of systematic inefficiencies can be documented, while the failure to detail such inefficiencies cannot prove efficiency. Still, in making judgments about the performance of speculation, knowledge of the results of such studies is useful.

The results of this type of empirical work to date are somewhat mixed. By and large, however, they suggest that there may well have been fairly widespread speculative inefficiencies during the early part of the float, but that if there were, these were substantially reduced or eliminated as the float progressed. The extent of speculative inefficiencies in the earlier part of the float is open to some question. One finds, for instance, that corresponding to the early fluctuations in the dollar–German mark exchange rate, numerous simple filter rules would have yielded substantial profits, suggesting the absence of sufficiently well behaved speculation. But over a longer period, one finds that many of the rules which would have made profits in the first stage, would then make losses.

Such results could be consistent with substantial initial inefficiencies which were remedied as the market adjusted to floating rates; or they could imply that speculation behaved efficiently all along but that underlying factors happened to vary in such a way that several successive cycles in the rate were generated. For example, *ex post* one can find many examples of cycles in stock prices even though a massive amount of statistical evidence has been accumulated to show that these prices are not dominated by inefficient speculation. Under either interpretation, however, the empirical results which cover longer experience with floating suggest that the major foreign exchange markets do not appear to have been characterized by a persistence of systematically poorly behaved speculation. I have derived a similar view on balance from my discussions with exchange market participants.[14]

eds., *Exchange-Rate Flexibility;* and Richard J. Sweeney, "Report on Technical Studies on Speculation and Market Efficiency," in Jacob Dreyer, Gottfried Haberler, and Thomas D. Willett, eds., *Flexible Exchange Rates and the International Monetary System* (Washington, D.C.: American Enterprise Institute, forthcoming).

[14] This statement is based on discussions between Treasury staff and foreign exchange market participants. A sample of views was presented at the Joint Treasury-American Enterprise Institute Conference on Flexible Exchange Rates in April 1976 and will appear in the conference volume. See especially John Rutledge's report on interviews with a number of exchange market participants,

Of course, such findings would still be consistent with the existence of occasional outbreaks of destabilizing speculation or of instances in which private speculation proved insufficient to smooth out fully the effects of temporary shocks. A priori there would seem to be a good deal of plausibility to the view that at times there may be insufficient stabilizing speculation in the foreign exchange markets. The exchange markets are widely viewed as being quite specialized and complicated to understand, and they do not attract the broad participation from the general public and many types of financial institutions that is enjoyed by the stock markets. Similarly, while the major commercial banks have considerable expertise in the exchange markets, the amounts of open speculative positions they are willing to take themselves are usually quite limited. But on the other hand, many multinational corporations and international trading firms do have substantial exchange market expertise and do move huge amounts of funds internationally, both directly and through variations in the leading and lagging of payments. Despite the frequency with which the possibility of insufficient stabilizing speculation is discussed, relatively little substantive evidence in support of this view has been presented. For example, one of the leading advocates of this view, Ronald McKinnon, presents only evidence that many speculators are constrained in the size of the open position they are willing or able to take, and that many exchange rates have varied a great deal.[15] He presents no evidence that this volatility has resulted from insufficient speculation in the aggregate. The well-documented observation that many individual speculators are constrained need not imply that aggregate speculation is insufficient. It is only a necessary, but not a sufficient, condition.

"An Economist's View of the Foreign Exchange Market: Report on Interviews With West Coast Foreign Exchange Dealers," in Dreyer, Haberler, and Willett, eds., *Flexible Exchange Rates.*

One potential source of confusion between the comments of economists and foreign exchange traders should also be clarified. Generally when economists talk about bandwagons of self-feeding destabilizing speculation, they have in mind major movements in exchange rates of 5 or 10 or 20 percent over several weeks or months, such as the large apparent cycles in the dollar/DM exchange rate during 1973 and 1974. Foreign exchange dealers, however, frequently express concern about apparent bandwagons that are intraday movements of exchange rates of 1 percent or less. Such movements are of understandable importance to traders whose profit margins are considerably less than 1 percent, but they would seldom be noticed on exchange rate charts such as presented in figure 1. Contrary to my initial impression, we discovered that comments by foreign exchange traders that bandwagons occur all the time, do not necessarily mean that the trader believes that speculation has been a major cause of the large cycles in exchange rates.

[15] McKinnon, "Floating Exchange Rates."

Proponents of the insufficient speculation hypothesis have in fact usually not even discussed how one would go about actually attempting to test this hypothesis. It is clear that there are fairly tight limitations placed by top management on the size of open foreign exchange positions taken by U.S. banks. There are similar management and/or government limitations imposed in many other countries as well. A large amount of the effective speculation or prudent risk avoidance in most foreign exchange markets, however, takes place through variations in the leads and lags associated with commercial payments. While again there are definite limits to the size of open positions of individual companies, the scope for aggregate open positions is considerable.

It is likewise not appropriate to take discussions of the thinness of foreign exchange markets during particular episodes as necessarily being evidence of insufficient stabilizing speculation. Frequently, thin exchange markets are the result of rational responses to a high degree of uncertainty. Constraints or limitations on the size of speculative positions are not the only reason why the elasticity of speculative funds may be quite low at times.

To establish the existence of seriously insufficient stabilizing speculation, it should be shown that there has been a strong consensus among informed experts and market participants that the current exchange rate is substantially overvalued or undervalued, but that speculators have been constrained from taking sufficiently large positions to close the gap between the current and future expected exchange rate. Although such a test is difficult to make operational in any precise sense, advocates of the insufficient stabilizing speculation hypothesis should be obligated to offer at least some evidence in support of their view.

One possibility would be to attempt to identify episodes in which the financial press reports the views of many experts and market participants that the level of an exchange rate is too high or too low, without any significant number of opposing views being expressed. For example, the precipitous decline of the pound below two dollars would clearly not pass even this weak presumptive test. While many officials, experts, and traders were reported as saying that the decline had been substantially overdone and the pound was undervalued, many others were predicting still greater declines. While there were complaints of excessive thinness of the market, this was not an episode in which the decline was due to the inability of a consensus of informed stabilizing speculators to take sufficiently large open positions to move the exchange rate to the level they thought was correct.

On the other hand, the sharp decline in the dollar in 1973 after the second devaluation and the initiation of generalized floating may well have been due in part to insufficient stabilizing speculation. This was a period in which many experts and traders expressed the view that the dollar had become undervalued without their being disputed by any substantial number of informed speculators. Indeed, it would not be at all surprising to find such occurrences at the beginning of the float, as the market was adjusting to the new circumstances. While I have not undertaken an exhaustive search for other episodes that would meet the suggested test for the possibility of insufficient stabilizing speculation, later episodes that would be strong candidates appear to be fairly rare.

Similarly, as noted above, the available empirical studies have generally failed to find the types of exchange rate patterns which would be consistent with major systematic speculative insufficiencies. It thus seems unlikely that the major cause of the variability of exchange rates under the current float can be attributed to an insufficiency of stabilizing speculation, at least after the early days of the float.

We do not have sufficiently robust models of the major foreign exchange markets to be able to say with confidence that virtually all the fluctuations in exchange rates can be explained in terms of efficient speculative responses to underlying variables and expectations of future developments; but neither can the opposite be shown.[16]

[16] A considerable amount of work is currently underway which should help to narrow, at least somewhat, our range of ignorance in this area. A number of papers have recently focused on the important influence of variations in monetary policy on exchange rates. See, for example, Rudiger Dornbusch, "The Theory of Flexible Exchange Rate Regimes and Macroeconomic Policy," pp. 255–75; Michael Mussa, "The Exchange Rate, the Balance of Payments and Monetary and Fiscal Policy Under a Regime of Controlled Floating," pp. 229–48; and Pentti J. K. Kouri, "The Exchange Rate and the Balance of Payments in the Short Run and in the Long Run: A Monetary Approach," pp. 280–304, all in *Scandinavian Journal of Economics*, vol. 78, no. 2 (1976); Rudiger Dornbusch, "Expectations and Exchange Rate Dynamics," *Journal of Political Economy*, vol. 84, no. 6 (December 1976), pp. 161–76; and U.S. Congress, International Economic Subcommittee of the Joint Economic Committee, "Problems of Monetary Reforms and Exchange Rate Management," 94th Congress, 1st session, July 18, 1975. Subsequent work by Arndt, Ethier, and Pigott and Sweeney suggests that the formulations of these models have in general led to overstatements of the degree to which monetary policy contributes to exchange rate variability. There can be little doubt, however, that variations in and uncertainties about monetary policies have been one of the important factors contributing to the variability of exchange rates. See Sven Arndt, "On Exchange Rate Dynamics" (Paper delivered at the Fourth Paris-Dauphine Conference, November 1–3, 1976), in E. Claassen and P. Salin, eds., *Asymmetries in the International Economy*, forthcoming; Wilfred Ethier, "Expectations and Asset-Market Theories of the Exchange Rate," University of Pennsylvania Discussion Paper no. 348 (May 1976);

Some leading experts have offered the opinion that the amount of exchange rate variability has not been excessive, given the underlying conditions,[17] whereas others have judged that taking such factors into account still leaves a significant portion of exchange rate variability unexplained.[18] There is, however, little disagreement that a major portion of this variability has been due to the underlying economic and financial conditions in the world economy.

Effects on International Trade and Resource Allocation

Traditionally it was widely believed that floating exchange rates would seriously harm international trade. Indeed as noted above, many critics had predicted that adoption of floating rates would cause a substantial decline in world trade. Our recent experiences with floating have strongly contradicted such dire fears. Whatever harmful effects floating may have on international trade have clearly been quite limited. Trade flows have not shown a significant decline from the levels that would normally be expected on the basis of

---

and Charles Pigott and Richard Sweeney, "International Price Dynamics" (in preparation). For a review and analysis of the literature on monetary policy and exchange rate dynamics, see Arndt and Pigott, "Monetary Policy and Exchange Rates," in Sweeney and Willett, eds., *Exchange-Rate Flexibility*. These papers show that in some popular models, variations in the money supply will cause more than proportionate variations in the exchange rate with the initial short-term adjustments overshooting the new long-run equilibrium rate. It should be emphasized, however, that these findings do not necessarily indicate deficiencies in the operation of floating rates, as would be the case with respect to the more common discussion of overshooting in terms of bandwagon effects or other types of flawed speculative behavior. The models used to show overshooting in the foreign exchange market in response to changes in monetary and fiscal policy are generally based on the assumption of efficient speculation in the foreign exchange market. The overshooting in the exchange rate is the counterpart of the tendency in most standard macroeconomic models for the initial changes in interest rates in response to a change in the rate of monetary growth to be greater than the longer run change. For example, in the latter models, after an initial fall in response to monetary expansion, interest rates would rise at least part way back toward their original levels. In models where there is efficient speculation in the domestic economy, the tendency for both interest rates and exchange rates to overshoot disappears. Thus, in practice, any tendency toward systematic overshooting of exchange rates in response to variations in monetary policy would be as or more likely to be the result of the nature of the adjustment process in the domestic economy than to be the result of deficiencies in the behavior of private speculators in the foreign exchange market.

[17] See, for example, Harry G. Johnson, "World Inflation and the International Monetary System," *The Three Banks Review*, no. 107 (September 1975), pp. 3–23.

[18] See, for example, E. M. Bernstein, "Fluctuating Exchange Rates," in Dreyer, Haberler, and Willett, eds., *Flexible Exchange Rates*.

changes in domestic economic activity.[19] Transaction costs in the foreign exchange market remain several times above their normal levels during the 1960s, but they have dropped substantially from their levels in the early days of generalized floating.[20] And even at these peaks, for the major currencies they amounted to only a small fraction of 1 percent. Furthermore, as with the volatility of exchange rates, these seem to be a function more of the degree of stability of underlying conditions than of the exchange rate system. Thus it seems unlikely that the adoption of floating rates per se has substantially increased the cost of international transactions.

Of course one still frequently hears complaints that floating is making life more difficult for this or that bank or business engaged in international activities. But there is no longer preponderant support among international bankers and businessmen for the par value system in preference to floating rates. Indeed recent congressional testimony by the National Association of Manufacturers suggests that a substantial majority of America's major business firms favors continuation of floating.[21] The main reason given for this favorable attitude was the belief that floating has removed the substantial overvaluation of the dollar which had developed under the Bretton Woods par value system, thus eliminating the retarding effects on U.S. exports and stimulation of U.S. imports. In addition, businessmen have found that the difficulties of operating under floating rates are not as great as many had anticipated.

---

[19] See, for example, John H. Makin, "Euro-Currencies and the Evolution of the International Monetary System," in Carl H. Stem, John H. Makin, and Dennis L. Logue, eds., *Eurocurrencies and the International Monetary System* (Washington, D.C.: American Enterprise Institute, 1976), pp. 31–34. See also Peter Hooper and Steven W. Kohlhagen, "The Effect of Exchange Rate Uncertainty on the Price and Volume of International Trade," Federal Reserve Board, International Finance Discussion Paper no. 91 (November 1976). Studies on the earlier Canadian experience during the 1950s yield similar results. See Leland Yeager, *International Monetary Relations: Theory, History, and Policy* (New York: Harper and Row, 1976), chap. 12, and Marie Thursby, "The Resource Reallocation Costs of Fixed and Flexible Exchange Rates: The Canadian Case," (paper presented at the Treasury Workshop on Exchange Rate Flexibility, February 1976).

[20] See, for example, Paul Volcker, president of the Federal Reserve Bank of New York, "The International Exchange Rate System: Problems, Progress, and Challenge" (Address delivered to the Conference Board in Toronto, Canada, June 24, 1976). For a review of the behavior of transactions costs since the move to floating, see Steven W. Kohlhagen, "The Behavior of Transactions Costs and Forward Rates Under Floating" in Sweeney and Willett, eds., *Exchange-Rate Flexibility*.

[21] Testimony of the National Association of Manufacturers before the House Committee on Banking, Currency, and Housing, Subcommittee on International Trade, Investment, and Monetary Policy, 94th Congress, 2nd session, June 1976.

This favorable view stems from a growing realization that the difficulties of operating under floating rates must be compared not with some ideal system but with realistic alternatives such as the adjustable peg and associated uncertainties of occasional large changes in par values and tendencies toward greater use of controls. Earlier, critics had frequently thought in terms of comparisons between wildly fluctuating exchange rates and an idealized fixed rate system, always at equilibrium and free of controls and of manipulation of domestic macroeconomic policies for balance-of-payments reasons. But, as Frank Graham pointed out in 1940 to those who asserted that floating rates would harm international trade and finance,

> . . . the choice is not between permanently fixed and fluctuating exchange rates but between temporary stability, subject to the shock of sharp change, and a more or less even fluctuation.[22]

The pressure of events such as the increasing frequency of exchange crises and the eventual devaluation of the pound in 1967 did much to force greater recognition that the par value system fell far short of the ideal of a fixed rate regime. This shift in perceptions substantially reduced the opposition to greater flexibility from men of practical affairs.

Of course, some critics of floating would today argue that casting the case for greater flexibility in terms of a preference for frequent small adjustments to occasional large ones was itself a false compari-

---

[22] Frank Graham, "Achilles Heel." Friedman in his classic article, "Flexible Exchange Rates," argues that "The substitution of flexible for rigid exchange rates changes the form in which uncertainty in the foreign exchange market is manifested; it may not change the extent of uncertainty at all and, indeed, may even decrease uncertainty. For example, conditions that would tend to produce a decline in a flexible exchange rate will produce a shortage of exchange with a rigid exchange rate. This in turn will produce either internal adjustments of uncertain character or administrative allocation of exchange" (p. 174). A similar argument is made by James Meade in his famous article on floating written in 1955, where he noted that those who charged that flexible rates increased the risks and uncertainties of foreign trade, ignored the risks that were reduced by floating, particularly the risks of controls over trade and payments. He went on to point out that floating "spreads the necessary adjustments all round at the margins of all exports and all imports with all countries, whereas the use of large and sudden variations in the quotas for particular products from particular countries concentrates the whole adjustment on one set of people—the choice of victims being, however, unsettled until the bureaucrats make their final decisions" (Meade, "Variable Exchange Rates," pp. 16–17). Egon Sohmen was one of the most forceful advocates of the need to distinguish between the adjustable peg and genuinely fixed rates. See Egon Sohmen, *Flexible Exchange Rates*, rev. ed. (Chicago: University of Chicago Press, 1969).

son. A look at the experience with floating during the 1970s might suggest that it represented the worst of both alternatives: many large changes. But to the extent that the volatility of exchange rates under floating has been a result of underlying factors, rather than of poorly behaved speculation, this is not a fair charge. Earlier comparisons of frequent small changes with occasional large ones were based on the implicit assumption that one was discussing the relatively stable economic conditions of the 1950s and of most of the 1960s.

For a long time during the postwar period, discussions of floating rates also tended to ignore the positive effects which exchange rate variations could have on resource allocation through preventing the emergence of distorted price signals resulting from the maintenance of exchange rates at disequilibrium levels. It was widely assumed that exchange rate changes caused a corresponding change in economic incentives and a consequent reallocation of resources. This may have been due in part to thinking in terms of the adjustable peg, which could not freely move to compensate for differences in underlying macroeconomic factors, in combination with the use of Keynesian macro models in which the price level was assumed constant.

Gradually, however, it was realized that exchange rate movements could only be taken as direct indicators of uncertainty and incentives for the reallocation of resources if there were no changes in the equilibrium exchange rate. Friedrich Lutz was one of the first to explain clearly how the maintenance of constant exchange rates in the face of divergent national inflation rates could lead to a distortion of price signals and a resulting misallocation of resources.[23]

As was argued in a recent paper by Pigott, Sweeney, and Willett:

> If exchange rate fluctuations are primarily a manifestation of developments and uncertainties arising in other sectors of the world economy, then attempts to peg currency values, while they may change the apparent distribution of risks arising from uncertainty, may not reduce the overall risks facing international traders, much less the economy as a whole. Indeed, exchange rate variations may well reduce the risks faced by some international traders and investors by on average partially offsetting fluctua-

---

[23] Friedrich A. Lutz, "Money Rates of Interest, Real Rates of Interest, and Capital Movements," in Fellner, et al., *Maintaining and Restoring Balance*, pp. 161–67. See also the important article by Richard Caves, "Flexible Exchange Rates," *American Economic Review: Papers and Proceedings*, vol. 53, no. 2 (May 1963), pp. 120–29. More recent treatments include Robert M. Dunn, *Exchange-Rate Rigidity, Investment Distortions, and the Failure of Bretton Woods*, Princeton Essays in International Finance no. 97 (February 1974); and Tower and Willett, *Optimum Currency Areas*, chap. 2.

tions in prices or other variables originating in other sectors. For instance, if a significant reason why exchange rates move is to offset movements in inter-country relative price levels, flexible rates may represent less actual risk for international traders and investors than would a fixed rate system even apart from whatever additional risks might be imparted by attempts to maintain fixed rates via controls, variation in macroeconomic policy, et cetera.[24]

Under the current float, exchange rate fluctuations may well have on average increased the combined price and exchange rate risk for activities which have a time horizon of a few months or less, but I would suspect that for the bulk of international economic and financial activity which has a considerably longer effective time horizon, the movements of floating rates on balance have had favorable effects on the efficiency of resource allocation.[25]

For the major currencies, there are active forward markets for the shorter time durations. Thus, forward markets are able to reduce substantially the risks for the types of activities that are most likely to face greater uncertainty under floating.[26] This further strengthens the judgment that on balance the adjustable peg is likely to have less favorable effects on the efficiency of resource allocation than are floating rates, even if one believes that a good bit of the variability of floating rates has been due to speculative deficiencies, rather than to underlying economic and financial conditions.

It should also be noted that the potential adverse effects of "excessive" exchange rate variability are frequently greatly exaggerated. Many critics of floating have falsely assumed that resources are

---

[24] Charles Pigott, Richard J. Sweeney, and Thomas D. Willett, "Some Aspects of the Behavior and Effects of Floating Rates" (Paper presented to the Conference on Monetary Theory and Policy, Konstanz, Germany, June 1975), available as U.S. Treasury Research Discussion Paper no. 75/31.

[25] For further discussion of the importance of considering the effective time horizon of activities in judging the effects of exchange rate variations on the efficiency of resource allocation, see Marie Thursby and Thomas D. Willett, "The Effects of Flexible Exchange Rates on International Trade and Investment," in Sweeney and Willett, eds., Exchange-Rate Flexibility.

[26] It is quite true that, as many critics have pointed out, exchange risk under floating rates cannot be entirely eliminated through the use of forward markets. But this is also true of any other realistic exchange rate system. It should also be noted that the absence of forward markets for particular maturities is not necessarily an indication of inefficiency. On this point see Johnson, "World Inflation and the International Monetary System," pp. 10–14. Many discussions greatly exaggerate the role of the forward market in reducing exchange risk. In practice, only a small portion of the hedging and covering activities of international firms takes place in the forward market.

always adjusted to changes in the exchange rate as if the new rate were expected with confidence to hold permanently. Thus, they argue that fluctuations in the exchange rate would be accompanied by a costly wrenching of resources back and forth, resulting in chaotic conditions. Such scenarios are highly exaggerated, however, for they would imply that in situations of frequently changing prices economic actors would react to each new price as if it were certain to be permanent. Experience under the float has not borne out such fears. Where prices are highly variable the responsiveness of resource flows to any particular change in price tends to be dampened.

The fact that many critics of floating have greatly exaggerated the likely adverse impact on resource allocation, of course, does not mean that there are no costs to exchange rate volatility. Such volatility does reduce the information content of current prices and exchange rates, and this carries a cost.[27] But this would be expected to act more to discourage foreign trade relative to domestic trade[28] than to cause rapid shifts of resources back and forth. And unless this variability in exchange rates is due to poorly behaved speculation, the cost cannot be reduced by official intervention to peg the exchange rate.

In well behaved markets, the variability in prices and exchange rates is the symptom, not the cause, of uncertainty and instability. In such markets, the key to exchange rate stability is the stability and degree of harmonization of underlying conditions among countries. International trade will inevitably be riskier between countries which have greatly disparate macroeconomic policies than between countries with more similar underlying economic conditions.[29] This holds regardless of the exchange rate system.

---

[27] Even if at each moment in time prices reflected the best mean estimate of future price developments, the variance of expected outcomes would widen, thus reducing the degree of confidence in allocative decisions based on current prices. Where adjustment costs are important, the short run responsiveness of resource allocation to changes in prices will be reduced.

[28] Even this result is not clearcut because while *ceteris paribus* foreign trade may be viewed as riskier than domestic trade, the effects of the covariance between domestic and foreign developments on the overall profitability of the firm should also be considered. Thus, it is possible for some developments that increase the expected variability of profits in foreign relative to domestic trade to lead nevertheless to increased incentives for foreign trade because of the effects on the covariances of profits between foreign and domestic trade.

[29] In this context, the term *disparate* has more than one dimension. For example, trade between two countries with large but relatively steady differences in rates of inflation might be a good deal less risky than between countries that had similar average rates of inflation but displayed considerable variability around this average.

How closely should various countries harmonize their macroeconomic policies to help facilitate international trade and investment? We are a long way from being able to answer this type of question with any great deal of confidence. Indeed, there is much we do not know about optimal strategies for macroeconomic policies based even on domestic considerations alone. And in recent years both actual macroeconomic experience and increased theoretical recognition of the role of expectations in influencing macroeconomic behavior have made us realize that we really know less than we thought we did ten years ago.[30] Thus, it is quite difficult on first-best theoretical grounds to reach firm judgments about the optimal degree of integration of macroeconomic policies among countries, taking into account effects both on international resource allocation and on domestic macroeconomic considerations.

It does seem clear, however, that most major countries are not going to be willing, within the foreseeable future, to give up a great deal of autonomy in macroeconomic policy, whatever might be optimal in strictly economic terms. Even though the once prevalent extremes of fine tuning discretionary macroeconomics have fallen out of favor, there are still enough apparent differences in underlying trends in the major economies to make it unlikely, and probably also unwise, for even fairly steady secular macroeconomic policies to be internationally determined.

Once a desire for independently determined macroeconomic policies is acknowledged, then, unless speculation is poorly behaved, floating rates become the most efficient exchange rate system in terms of both resource allocation and resource utilization. Where private speculation is imperfect, the question becomes one of the optimal mix of imperfect private and public speculation. It is not possible to make definitive universal judgments on this mix. From this perspective, however, it is extremely unlikely that the type of strategy of public speculation implied by the adjustable peg system would receive high marks.

This conclusion holds as well for arguments based on enhancing the usefulness of international money. It is sometimes implied that floating rate advocates do not appreciate the usefulness of money and

---

[30] For reviews of the current state of macroeconomic theory in this regard, see William Fellner, *Towards a Reconstruction of Macroeconomics* (Washington, D.C.: American Enterprise Institute, 1976); Robert Gordon, "Recent Developments in the Theory of Inflation and Unemployment," *Journal of Monetary Economics*, vol. 2, no. 2 (April 1976); and John Rutledge, "The Unemployment-Inflation Trade-Off—A Review Article," *Claremont Economic Papers*, no. 141 (July 1975).

are opposed to international money.[31] To the contrary, I would argue that given the unlikely prospects for full integration of monetary policies, floating rates represent the best practical means of facilitating the usefulness of money internationally by reducing the use of controls and the maintenance of disequilibrium rates of exchange.[32] It is certainly not true that advocates of floating rates have overlooked the effects of alternative exchange rate systems on the usefulness of money.[33] Analytically the criteria for evaluation on this score are the same as in the general discussion of the microeconomic efficiency effects of international trade and investment. Added to this in today's world is the second-best consideration, emphasized by Keynes, Fisher, and Graham many years ago,[34] that where there is not monetary stability abroad, exchange rate flexibility is essential to facilitate monetary stability at home.

In summary, while we must be quite modest in our claims of knowledge about the effects of floating on international trade and investment and the efficiency of resource allocation, I would judge that floating rates should receive relatively good marks on this score. They certainly have not imposed the huge costs anticipated by many opponents of floating.

Balance-of-Payments Adjustment

Another major area of criticism of the performance of floating rates concerns the adjustment process. At the most naive level, some have

---

[31] See, for example, Charles P. Kindleberger, "The Benefits of International Money," *Journal of International Economics*, vol. 2, no. 4 (September 1972), pp. 425–42.

[32] Some critics of floating argue that floating rates will generate more use of controls and that in a world of floating rates laws against the use of other currencies will be required for most countries to keep domestic currencies in circulation. See, for example, Arthur B. Laffer, "Two Arguments for Fixed Exchange Rates," in Harry G. Johnson and Alexander K. Swoboda, eds., *The Economics of Common Currencies* (Cambridge: Harvard University Press, 1973), pp. 25–34.

Such arguments are usually cast in terms of comparisons between floating and genuinely fixed rates. It is not at all clear that a move from an adjustable peg system to a well-functioning system of floating rates would diminish the viability of domestic currencies, however. In my judgment, this school of critics of floating frequently tends to exaggerate greatly the extent of the economic pressures toward a single world money. I would judge the number of optimum currency areas in the world to be considerably greater than would critics such as Kindleberger, Laffer, and Mundell.

[33] See, for example, Harry G. Johnson, "The Case for Flexible Exchange Rates, 1969," in Halm, ed., *Approaches to Greater Flexibility*, pp. 91–111; John Makin, "Eurocurrencies"; and Tower and Willett, *Optimum Currency Areas*, chap. 2.

[34] See the discussion on this in chapter 1.

criticized floating rates for not eliminating all trade or current account imbalances.[35] Such charges fail to recognize that the role of exchange rate adjustments is to eliminate overall payments imbalances, not to balance some particular subset of the accounts.

An only slightly less naive criticism of floating rates is that they are not a panacea for balance-of-payments adjustment problems; that they do not eliminate all the costs of correcting payments imbalances or all the adverse foreign exchange rate consequences of domestic inflation and economic and financial instability. Again, however, this is hardly a reasonable expectation. In most instances all floating rates can do is to reduce the costs of adjustment as compared with other alternatives and to reduce the probability of serious disequilibrium emerging, but that is all that can be reasonably expected of the addition of another policy instrument.

A third and more serious form of criticism is that exchange rate adjustments no longer work, that they cannot be counted upon to bring about balance-of-payments adjustment. Such a view has been most closely associated with the names of Robert Mundell and Art Laffer,[36] but has to some degree also been (falsely) associated with the whole school of theorists who emphasize the monetary approach to the balance of payments.

Laffer presents both empirical and theoretical attacks on the effectiveness of exchange rate adjustments as an instrument of balance-of-payments adjustment. His empirical argument emphasizes that there are many instances in which exchange rate adjustments have not been accompanied by reductions in trade imbalances. But as pointed out by a number of commentators on Laffer's work in a 1974 Treasury-sponsored conference on exchange rate adjustments,[37] this finding is hardly strong evidence against the effectiveness of exchange rate adjustments, for no attempt was made to hold constant the effects of many other factors. The many empirical studies that have attempted to take into account the effects of other major influences affecting the

---

[35] See, for example, the comments reported in the article "The Drift Back to Fixed Exchange Rates," *Business Week* (June 2, 1975), pp. 60–63. This article contains a useful compendium of some of the more exaggerated criticisms of floating.

[36] See Arthur B. Laffer, "The Bitter Fruits of Devaluation," *Wall Street Journal* (January 10, 1974); Laffer, "Do Devaluations Really Help Trade?" *Wall Street Journal* (February 5, 1973); and Jude Wanniski, "The Mundell-Laffer Hypothesis— A New View of the World Economy," *The Public Interest*, no. 39 (Spring 1975), pp. 31–52.

[37] See Peter B. Clark, Dennis E. Logue, and Richard J. Sweeney, eds., *The Effects of Exchange Rate Adjustments* (Washington, D.C.: U.S. Government Printing Office, 1977).

balance of payments generally do find a significant positive impact of exchange rate changes on adjustment.[38]

Laffer and Mundell rest their case primarily on the "law of one price," which states that identical goods tend not to differ in price from one place to another except by transportation costs. Laffer and Mundell correctly argue that if all goods were perfect substitutes, exchange rate changes would not affect relative prices, but would affect only national price levels. Laffer has also extensively documented the fact that the markets for a number of internationally traded goods, such as many raw materials, do behave in this manner.[39] Then, however, comes the illegitimate leap to the implicit assumption that all markets behave this way.

A high proportion of internationally traded products are industrial and consumer goods that are not homogeneous, and there are many goods and services that for all practical purposes are not traded internationally at all.[40] Laffer and Mundell are correct when they stress that exchange rate adjustments will directly affect the prices not only of goods actually exported and imported but also of domestically produced and sold goods that are identical or close substitutes, and that calculations ignoring this will tend to understate the effects of exogenous exchange rate adjustment on prices. The Mundell-Laffer hypothesis, however, greatly exaggerates the magnitude of this effect, at least for the major industrial countries.

It should be noted that this type of argument by Laffer and Mundell about the alleged ineffectiveness of exchange rate adjustment runs directly counter to the similar concerns expressed in the early postwar period by the elasticity pessimists. The latter were concerned that the effects of exchange rate adjustments would be perverse because of a very low degree of substitutability among commodities. The Mundell-Laffer argument is that they will not work because of an almost infinite degree of substitutability. While both are logically valid theoretical possibilities,[41] neither set of empirical assumptions

---

[38] Ibid.

[39] See Arthur B. Laffer, "The Phenomenon of Worldwide Inflation," in David I. Meiselman and Arthur B. Laffer, eds., *The Phenomenon of Worldwide Inflation* (Washington, D.C.: American Enterprise Institute, 1975), pp. 27–57.

[40] For a recent extensive review of the empirical studies of international price elasticities, see Robert M. Stern, J. H. Francis, and B. Schumacher, *Price Elasticities in International Trade* (London: Macmillan Press, 1976). See also Peter Isard, "How Far Can We Push the 'Law of One Price'?," Federal Reserve Board, International Finance Discussion Paper no. 84 (May 1976) and the discussions on this subject in Clark, Logue, and Sweeney, eds., *Exchange Rate Adjustments*.

[41] In his paper in Clark, Logue, and Sweeney, eds., *Exchange Rate Adjustments*, Laffer presents a theoretical model in which it is extremely difficult to find conditions for devaluation to improve the balance of payments. As was pointed out

explains the actual behavior of exchange rates and balance-of-payments developments under the current float.

Two sets of theoretical arguments often associated with those who write on the monetary approach to the balance of payments have also been used to argue against the efficacy of exchange rate adjustment. One is that exchange rate adjustments cannot work without money or exchange illusion and that today there is little such illusion left; hence the traditional case for exchange rate adjustments has been undercut. I shall not attempt to discuss how much money and exchange illusion, if any, may be left in today's world. It must be emphasized, however, that while many treatments of the effects of exchange rate adjustments have made use of the assumption of money illusion, the case for the efficacy of exchange rate adjustments is not dependent upon the existence of money illusion.[42]

The second set of arguments concerns two propositions that are correctly demonstrated in recent papers on the monetary approach.[43] One is that a one-shot, exchange rate adjustment is not sufficient to maintain balance-of-payments equilibrium in the face of a flow disequilibrium in the domestic economy. In other words, if one country's inflation rate is, say, 10 percent higher than another's, the resulting pressures for balance-of-payments equilibrium cannot be corrected by a one-time devaluation. Although this simple truism is hardly surprising to advocates of floating rates, it has been used by some critics as an argument against floating. The answer, of course, is that to achieve balance-of-payments equilibrium under such circumstances, there should be continuous exchange rate adjustment.

---

by several commentators at the conference, Laffer's model had left out what traditionally has been considered the most powerful part of price adjustment mechanisms—changes in the relative prices of traded and nontraded goods. Thus, Laffer's model really gave a graphic illustration of the importance of the mechanism that he had left out of his model.

[42] See, for example, William Fellner, "Controlled Floating and the Confused Issue of Money Illusion," *Banca Nazionale del Lavoro Quarterly Review*, no. 106 (September 1973), pp. 206–33; Ronald I. McKinnon, "Exchange Rate Flexibility"; Gottfried Haberler, *Economic Growth and Stability* (Los Angeles: Nash Publishers, 1974), pp. 186, 271–73; and Sweeney and Willett, "The Inflationary Effects of Exchange Rate Changes," in Clark, Logue, and Sweeney, eds., *Exchange Rate Adjustments*.

[43] Many of the papers on the monetary approach are conveniently collected in Jacob A. Frenkel and Harry G. Johnson, eds., *The Monetary Approach to the Balance of Payments* (Toronto: University of Toronto Press, 1976). See also the very cogent review of this volume by Gottfried Haberler in *The Journal of Economic Literature*, vol. 14, no. 4 (December 1976), pp. 1324–28, and Marina Whitman's review paper, "Global Monetarism and the Monetary Approach to the Balance of Payments," *Brookings Papers on Economic Activity*, no. 3 (1975), pp. 491–555.

A related proposition from the monetary approach is that if a devaluation of the exchange rate is considered from a position of full equilibrium, then full monetary equilibrium will not be restored until the balance of payments has returned to its initial equilibrium. Again, this proposition is true, but hardly novel;[44] and it cannot be legitimately used, as it sometimes has been used, to conclude that exchange rate adjustments are therefore not an effective balance-of-payments policy. The proposition does indicate that an exchange rate adjustment cannot be used to create a permanent disequilibrium in the balance of payments. But that is not a legitimate objective of balance-of-payments policy in the first place. The appropriate role of exchange rate adjustments is not to create disequilibrium but to keep disequilibrium from emerging or to correct disequilibriums that have already been generated. The inability of exchange rate adjustments to create permanent disequilibriums tells nothing about their ability to restore and maintain equilibrium.[45]

Finally, there is concern over the effects of floating rates as regards the short-run operation of the so-called J-curve effect. In the short run, trade elasticities tend to be fairly low, and discreet devaluations have frequently worsened the trade balance for a period of time before higher longer run elasticities come into play and the trade balance begins to improve; that is, the trade balance responds in a J-like fashion. Coupled with the absence of stabilizing speculation, this could lead to overshooting and instability in the foreign exchange market.

While there has been much discussion of the theoretical possibilities of overshooting, I know of no careful studies indicating that speculative reactions to J-curve effects have actually caused serious exchange market instability. Since the market well understands J-curve effects by now, any such temporary worsening in the trade balance is unlikely to adversely affect speculative expectations. Although it has not been demonstrated, a more plausible tendency would be for some instability to result from insufficient stabilizing speculation to offset this temporary effect.

In part, the absence of widespread adverse consequences from J-curve effects may be due to the fact, often not fully recognized, that the J-curve would only be expected to operate when real adjustments to trade flows must be induced. Where exchange rate move-

---

[44] There is, for example, a good discussion of the proposition that balance-of-payments disequilibrium is inconsistent with full domestic monetary equilibrium, in the first edition of Yeager's *International Monetary Relations*, pp. 76–77.

[45] For a more extensive discussion of these points, see Sweeney and Willett, "The Inflationary Effects of Exchange Rate Adjustment."

ments are offsetting other factors—that is, where they are preventing the emergence of disequilibrium—then J-curve effects are not induced. Concern about the consequences of J-curve effects may have been due in large part to failure to shift thinking from the old system of occasional direct exchange rate adjustments to our new system of greater exchange rate flexibility.

It should likewise be noted that finding the process of real adjustment of trade patterns to be more difficult and slower than originally expected is not an argument against exchange rate flexibility.[46] It rather increases the importance of keeping disequilibrium from emerging as the result of over- or under-valued exchange rates and hence strengthens the importance of having flexible exchange rates.

Insulation and Policy Independence

Floating exchange rates cannot fully shield countries from all macroeconomic developments in other countries. However, few, if any, serious advocates of floating rates were guilty of asserting that floating rates would completely insulate an economy from all types of disturbances abroad and give domestic monetary and fiscal policy as great a degree of independence from international developments as could be obtained in a closed economy. Friedman was quite careful, as were most subsequent writers, to point out that floating rates could not insulate any economy from all types of shocks.

Indeed, there is a huge volume of literature on the transmission of different types of economic disturbances under floating and on the insulating properties of alternative exchange rate systems.[47] The general thrust of this literature is that international capital mobility and stabilizing speculation tend to reduce the differences between pegged and floating rates in transmitting macroeconomic disturbances from one economy to another. A short, precise summary is not possible because there are many different transmission mechanisms, and particular outcomes will depend on the relative importance of the different mechanisms, the particular type of disturbance, and some of the major parameters of the economy in question.[48]

---

[46] See Thomas D. Willett, "International Payments Adjustment: Discussion," in Peter Kenen, ed., *International Trade and Finance* (London: Cambridge University Press, 1976), pp. 491–99.

[47] This literature is reviewed in chapter 5 of Tower and Willett, *Optimum Currency Areas.*

[48] For a review of the major transmission mechanisms, see Richard J. Sweeney and Thomas D. Willett, "The International Transmission of Inflation: Mechanisms, Issues and Evidence," Special Supplement on Money, Bank Credit, and Inflation in Open Economies, *Kredit und Kapital* (Heft 3, 1976), pp. 441–517.

While floating rates have not increased the speed and independence of monetary policy as greatly as had been implied by some of the literature on this subject,[49] they have clearly given countries greater control over domestic monetary aggregates; and in countries such as West Germany, this has been viewed as a major beneficial aspect of floating.[50] Even under freely floating rates, however, effects of monetary and fiscal policies may be transmitted through Keynesian trade balance effects. With sufficiently high capital mobility, the international transmission of some types of domestic disturbances can be even greater under floating than under fixed rates. In general, however, the degree of international capital mobility seems to be such that there is no strong presumption of either greater or smaller transmission of macroeconomic disturbances through the Keynesian mechanism of trade imbalances.[51]

It should be noted that such a result not only reduces the insulating properties of floating, but also tends to undercut such writers as Baffi, Bernstein, Laffer, Mundell, and Triffin in their argument that fixed rates foster stability by spreading out disturbances from the country of origin onto the world economy.[52] Such arguments are

---

[49] For reviews and evaluations of this literature, see Richard N. Cooper, "Monetary Theory and Policy in an Open Economy," *The Scandinavian Journal of Economics*, vol. 78, no. 2 (1976), pp. 146–65, and Thomas D. Willett, "The Eurocurrency Market, Exchange-Rate Systems, and National Financial Policies," in Stem, et al., eds., *Eurocurrencies*. Four more recent contributions on this subject are Robert Aliber, "Monetary Independence Under Floating Exchange Rates," *Journal of Finance*, vol. 30, no. 2 (May 1975), pp. 365–76; R. Dornbusch, "Exchange Rate Expectations and Monetary Policy," *Journal of International Economics*, vol. 6, no. 3 (August 1976), pp. 231–44; Peter B. Kenen, *Flexible Exchange Rates and National Autonomy* (Milan, Italy: Arti Grafiche Longo & Zoppelli, 1976); and J. Niehans, "Some Doubts About the Efficacy of Monetary Policy Under Flexible Exchange Rates," *Journal of International Economics*, vol. 5, no. 3 (August 1975), pp. 275–82.

[50] See, for example, Otmar Emminger, *On the Way to a New International Monetary Order* (Washington, D.C.: American Enterprise Institute, 1976), p. 8.

[51] See Willett, "The Eurocurrency Market," in Stem, et al., eds., *Eurocurrencies*, and Victoria S. Farrell, "Capital Mobility and the Efficacy of Fiscal Policy under Alternative Exchange-Rate Systems," in the same volume, pp. 234–48.

[52] See, for example, Paolo Baffi, "Western European Inflation and the Reserve Currencies," *Banca Nazionale del Lavoro Quarterly Review*, no. 84 (March 1968); E. M. Bernstein's comment in *International Payments Problems* (Washington, D.C.: American Enterprise Institute, 1966), pp. 83–87, and his essay, "Flexible Exchange Rates and International Adjustment," in Randall Hinshaw, ed., *The Economics of International Adjustment* (Baltimore: The Johns Hopkins University Press, 1971), pp. 157–58; Arthur B. Laffer, "Two Arguments for Fixed Rates," in Johnson and Swoboda, eds., *The Economics of Common Currencies*, pp. 25–33, and the critiques in the same volume by Bela Balassa (pp. 40–45) and Gottfried Haberler (pp. 35–39); Robert A. Mundell, "Uncommon Arguments for Common Currencies," in Johnson and Swoboda, eds., *The Economics of Common Currencies*, pp. 114–32; Robert Triffin, *Our International Monetary System:*

typically presented in terms of the example of the domestic stabilizing impact of the cyclical import surplus which would accompany a domestic boom. But as was discussed extensively by Friedman in his original 1950 article, private speculation and interest-sensitive capital flows would play the same role under floating rates. Indeed, Modigliani and Askari have recently argued that capital mobility is so high that the spreading out through this Keynesian mechanism will be greater under floating than under pegged rates.[53] Although Modigliani and Askari's conclusions on the degree of capital mobility do not at present have strong empirical support, they highlight questions about the applicability of the Baffi-Triffin type arguments as well.

The Modigliani-Askari article also underlines the difficulty of assessing the desirable degree of transmission of disturbances. Contrary to the Baffi-Triffin position, Modigliani and Askari maintain that such transmission should be minimized from the standpoint of all countries taken together. But this does not necessarily follow, because diversification may make some degree of transmission in the long-run interest of most countries.[54] On the other hand, maximizing transmission can give rise to severe problems of "moral hazard" by creating incentives for countries to export inflation. Without further research, our knowledge does not take us very far in judging the performance of floating rates in this area.

We should be equally modest about our understanding of short-term transmission through direct price effects. Many have criticized floating rates on this score because of the alleged operation of ratchet effects, et cetera, and the recognition that floating rates have been more volatile than have ex post inflation rate differentials. But it is clear that floating rates provide much greater insulation from differential price trends than the adjustable peg. By assuming steady rates of inflation, however, many discussions have exaggerated the degree to which floating rates would insulate countries from inflationary developments abroad. If country A inflates steadily at 20 percent a year while country B inflates at only 5 percent, then all that is required for full insulation is a 15 percent rate of appreciation for B's currency

Yesterday, Today and Tomorrow (New York: Random House, 1968), pp. 75–77; Haberler and Willett, *U.S. Balance of Payments Policies and International Monetary Reform*, p. 70; Tower and Willett, *Optimum Currency Areas;* and Willett, "The Eurocurrency Market," in Stem, et al., eds., *Eurocurrencies.*

[53] Franco Modigliani and Hossein Askari, "The International Transfer of Capital and the Propagation of Domestic Disturbances Under Alternative Payments Systems," *Banca Nazionale del Lavoro Quarterly Review,* no. 107 (December 1973), pp. 295–310.

[54] This is emphasized by several authors cited above who argue for pegged rates on what are essentially automatic stabilization grounds.

relative to A's. In such a world, under floating rates, countries would not be affected by each other's inflation, and a country's macroeconomic policies would be purely its own concern. The welfare costs of even quite high rates of inflation would be trivial, being almost entirely the welfare cost associated with the accompanying inflation tax on noninterest-bearing cash balances. But in actuality, high rates of inflation tend to be variable rather than steady and to increase substantially the underlying uncertainty and instability in the economy.[55]

The underlying macroeconomic uncertainty and instability are in turn reflected in volatile foreign exchange rates.[56] Thus, underlying instability in one country is still to some degree exported to other countries through the foreign exchange market, which explains continued international concern with individual countries' macroeconomic policies even under freely floating rates.

This is not necessarily an argument for official intervention. High inflation rates and accompanying uncertainty and instability in some countries mean that official intervention may be able to do little to limit the transmission of these instabilities. Indeed, attempts to manage exchange rates too heavily have themselves often generated additional instability. In a world where some major countries are inflating at 15 or 20 percent a year while others have virtually stable prices, it is hardly realistic to attempt to counter exchange rate fluctuations by orchestrating national monetary and fiscal policies, as is implied by those who argue that national interest rate policies should be used to offset short-term exchange market fluctuations.

Recognizing this, the Rambouillet and Jamaica agreements stress that greater exchange market stability depends on greater stability in the underlying economic and financial conditions.[57] Enduring exchange market stability cannot be imposed; it must be earned.

---

[55] See, for example, Dennis Logue and Thomas D. Willett, "A Note on the Relations Between the Rate and Variability of Inflation," *Economica*, vol. 43, no. 70 (May 1976), pp. 151–58, and references cited there.

[56] Important recent theoretical work on the dynamics of adjustment of exchange rates to variations in monetary and fiscal policy has greatly increased our understanding of the complexities of the short-run interrelationships between monetary and ficsal policies, expectations, and exchange rate dynamics. Three of the most important contributions to this literature by Dornbusch, Kouri, and Mussa respectively were presented at the Conference on Flexible Exchange Rates and Stabilization Policy and published in *The Scandinavian Journal of Economics*, vol. 78, no. 2 (1976). See also Dornbusch, "Expectations," and Arndt and Pigott, "Monetary Policy."

[57] This is discussed in greater detail in chapter 3.

Floating Exchange Rates, the Alleged Vicious Circle, and World Inflation

There are some myths which never seem to die. One of the most prevalent of these in the area of international economics is the belief that floating rates are inherently inflationary. Frequently such charges are not even coupled with the minimal analytical question, "as compared with what?"

Such charges also display a high propensity to confuse symptoms with causes. There is a long history of such fallacies, going back at least to the 1920s, when many commentators attempted to blame the German hyperinflation on destabilizing speculation and exchange rate depreciation.[58] Since then, even critics of floating have generally recognized that, in the absence of at least accommodating monetary expansion, exchange rate depreciation could not by itself set off a process of cumulative inflation and self-justifying depreciation. Thus, the crudest form of the alleged vicious circle of depreciation and inflation has been substantially put to rest. Many alternative versions, however, still abound.

As typically expounded in its modern version, the vicious-circle hypothesis goes something like the following: it is more difficult for countries to control inflation under flexible exchange rates because inflation causes exchange rate depreciation, which immediately boosts import costs. This in turn causes the aggregate price indices to rise, which causes further depreciation of the exchange rate; and the circle starts all over again.

While not always mentioned in the standard exposition, almost all modern advocates of this vicious-circle argument grant that such a cumulative circle would not go on and on unless validated by expansionary financial policies. Rather, they maintain that floating rates make reducing inflation more difficult and tend to widen the differences in inflation rates between high- and low-inflation countries. In other words, the charge is that floating rates cause additional inflation. Even in this revised form, the typical, modern vicious-circle arguments still confuse statistical and behavioral relationships, and they usually fail to distinguish between the systems of adjustable pegs and floating exchange rates.

Calculations of the inflationary impact of exchange rate depreciations are generally based on the mechanical relationship between import prices and aggregate price indices. For example, if import prices

---

[58] For an early critical analysis of such views, see Gottfried Haberler, *The Theory of International Trade* (London: W. Hodge and Co., 1936), pp. 44–46, 55–61.

carry a weight of 10 percent in a particular country's wholesale price index, then a 20 percent depreciation in the exchange rate, if fully reflected in higher import prices, would increase the domestic price index by 2 percent. More sophisticated calculations may also take into account impacts on the domestic prices of exported products and import substitutes, and induced reactions of wages as estimated from some macroeconometric model.

Despite their increased sophistication, these calculations share the same basic limitation as back-of-the-envelope calculations: they do not establish causation. Therefore, they can no more give insight into the validity of the vicious-circle hypothesis than can the well-established empirical correlation between high rates of inflation and depreciating exchange rates. Calculations of the mechanics of inflationary impacts tell us nothing about whether these price increases are caused by underlying inflationary pressures in the country in question or are the result of some capricious and unjustified movement in the exchange rate.[59]

Suppose, for example, that a country begins to inflate more rapidly than its neighbors. Then, *ceteris paribus*, the resulting demand and supply shifts will cause the equilibrium exchange rate to depreciate and observed import and export prices to rise. This decrease in exchange rate, however, is clearly the result of changes in underlying inflationary pressures, rather than the independent cause of inflation.

Consider the following simple example. In a simple quantity theory world with full employment and efficient speculation, expansion of the money supply by 10 percent will (in a closed economy) eventually lead to a 10 percent increase in prices. In an open economy with floating rates the same theory will apply; while domestic prices

---

[59] For further discussion, see Charles Pigott, John Rutledge, and Thomas D. Willett, "Analyzing the Interrelationships Between Inflation and Exchange Rate Movements: A Critique of the Vicious Circle Hypothesis," in Sweeney and Willett, eds., *Exchange-Rate Flexibility*. Strictly speaking it is not correct to speak of causation running from inflation to exchange rates or vice versa. Both exchange rates and prices are endogenous variables, determined by underlying factors such as monetary and fiscal policies, productivity growth, et cetera. When causation is said to run primarily from prices to exchange rates, what is really said is that the underlying macro variables that determine prices are also the main determinants of the exchange rate. Likewise, the statement that causation runs from exchange rates to inflation implies that the exchange rate change is exogenous to the domestic inflationary process. (Of course even in this case, the import price effects of the exchange rate change would have to be validated by domestic macroeconomic policies in order to influence significantly the overall price level). All empirical studies that I have seen on the effects of exchange rate changes on inflation assume that exchange rate changes are exogenous, which limits the value of these statistical results in analyzing the interrelationships between exchange rates and inflation under floating exchange rates.

are rising by 10 percent, import prices will also rise by 10 percent. If other countries are also inflating at 10 percent, then the increase in the home country's import prices will come directly from the increase in foreign exporters' prices with no change in the exchange rate. If, on the other hand, there is no inflation in the home country's trading partners, its import prices will still rise by 10 percent but this will be associated with a depreciation of its exchange rate by 10 percent.

While it can be said that in this case the exchange rate depreciation causes import price increases to keep up with the general level of inflation in a mechanical sense, it would clearly be wrong to use this mechanical relationship to place the blame for import price increases on the exchange rate depreciation. Nor would these import price increases be the cause of further exchange rate depreciation as is assumed in presentations of the vicious-circle hypothesis. The initial depreciation and import price increases would be the reflection of the already existing expansion in aggregate demand, not the cause of further inflation.

It is important to recognize that a change in relative inflation rates will tend to depreciate the equilibrium exchange rate even in a system of pegged exchange rates, because it will generate strictly analogous demand shifts and price pressures. If, by running down its foreign exchange reserves or by running up its international indebtedness, the country prevents the actual exchange rate from depreciating, it will succeed for a time in exporting its inflation to its trading partners and thus in holding down the extent of price increases. With finite reserves and borrowing power, however, the exchange rate adjustment required by the differential inflation rates cannot be postponed indefinitely. When actual and equilibrium exchange rates are finally aligned, import prices will rise; and these increases must properly be attributed not to devaluation but to the country's relatively higher inflation. It is ironic that in such instances countries frequently complain about importing back the inflation they had previously exported. There is, of course, an element of truth in the argument that floating rates complicate the life of inflation-prone countries: their ability to export inflationary pressures and thereby to extract subsidies from their neighbors is sharply circumscribed. From the standpoint of the international system as a whole, this must be viewed as a virtue rather than a vice.

Some proponents of the vicious-circle hypothesis would presumably grant that to the extent exchange rate depreciations are the direct result of domestic inflation, they cannot legitimately be labeled a cause of additional inflationary pressures. These proponents would go on to argue, however, that exchange rate depreciations are frequently exaggerated because of destabilizing speculation or other shifts in capital flows, and that these exaggerated depreciations are the cause of additional inflationary pressures. This more limited version of the vicious-circle hypothesis is on sounder analytic foundation. Various types of disturbances can certainly cause exchange rate movements under floating rates to alter short-run inflation-unemployment trade-offs from what they would be in a closed economy or in an open economy under fixed exchange rates.[60] Proponents of vicious-circle arguments have a tendency, however, to focus primarily on examples of the types of disturbances which worsen the inflation-unemployment trade-off in high inflation countries. And in making judgments about actual developments, they frequently assume that any large and rapid depreciation and any depreciation greater than inflation differentials are evidence of exaggerated or excessive exchange rate movements which cause a worsening of inflation-unemployment trade-offs.

Such criteria are seriously deficient, however. It is well established in modern economic analysis that the important role of expectations in economic behavior makes it difficult to infer causation from the leading or lagging relationship of one statistical series to another. Indeed, this point was applied specifically to the vicious-circle question by Gottfried Haberler more than forty years ago in his classic book, *The Theory of International Trade*, to explain why the building up of domestic inflationary pressures would be expected to lead to a depreciation of the exchange rate more rapid than the initial inflation in domestic prices. The lag in domestic prices behind the exchange rate depreciation, however, would not imply that causation ran from depreciation to domestic price increases.

This point is reinforced when it is recognized that in the context of the current float, the large variability of exchange rates has been, for many of the high-inflation countries, the legacy of periods of heavy official management which in many ways more closely approximated the old system of adjustably pegged exchange rates than a system of freely floating rates. Where heavy official intervention is used by highly inflationary countries for a long period of time to bolster their currencies artificially in the foreign exchange market, the reduction

---

[60] See, for example, Richard J. Sweeney and Thomas D. Willett, "Analyzing the Inflationary Impact of Alternative International Monetary Systems," in Sweeney and Willett, eds., *Exchange-Rate Flexibility* (an earlier version of this paper, "The International Transmission of Inflation," was presented by Sweeney and Willett at the Conference on Bank Credit, Money and Inflation in Open Economies, at Louvain, Belgium, September 1974).

or cessation of such official support will frequently result in large, rapid depreciations of the exchange rate well in excess of the difference in past inflation rates.

Not only may excessive official intervention artificially hold down domestic price increases and keep the exchange rate at too high a level, but the accumulation of the heavy international debts associated with such large-scale official intervention increases uncertainty in the foreign exchange market. These factors, coupled with the additional need to generate future payment surpluses to repay accumulated debt, make it not at all surprising that there have recently been some quite large and rapid movements in exchange rates. It is certainly not legitimate automatically to classify such movements as the result of exaggerated speculative behavior, or automatically to attribute the associated instabilities to floating exchange rates.

There is little doubt that, given the degree of underlying inflationary pressures, exchange rate adjustments would have been much prompter and smoother under relatively freely floating rates than they have been under adjustably pegged and heavily managed rates. Recognition of this is gradually spreading, but it will still take some time to work off the legacy of past heavy management of exchange rates. It may also be hoped that, by making it more difficult to disguise the initial effects of inflationary pressures, relatively freely floating rates will not only reduce instabilities in the foreign exchange market, but also provide greater discipline for governments to resist succumbing to the pressures to adopt inflationary policies.

There has been much discussion through the years of the role of the discipline of fixed exchange rates in discouraging inflationary policies. It is an open question whether exchange rate depreciation with freely floating rates or balance-of-payments deficits with genuinely fixed exchange rates would provide a stronger source of discipline against inflationary policies, but there can be little doubt that adjustably pegged or heavily managed exchange rate systems would score the lowest marks in this. An attempt to establish genuinely fixed exchange rates hardly would be realistic, even if desirable, which leaves floating rates as the best practical system for reducing a government's propensities to engage in inflationary policies.[61]

---

[61] As was concluded in the two papers on this topic presented at the Conference on Flexible Exchange Rates and Stabilization Policy, and published in the *Scandinavian Journal of Economics*, vol. 78, no. 2 (1976), when all, or even several, of the major ways in which exchange rate systems can influence inflation are taken into account, it is not possible to conclude that either genuinely fixed or floating rates are inherently more inflationary. See Emil-Maria Classen, "World Inflation Under Flexible Exchange Rates," and W. Max Corden, "Inflation and

As compared with adjustably pegged or heavily managed exchange rates, floating gives low-inflation countries greater ability to shield themselves against the inflationary policies of others and also reduces the inflationary pressures generated by massive international movements of capital in anticipation of exchange rate realignments. There can be no question that at times under floating rates private speculation will cause rates to depreciate "too far" as determined ex post, just as at other times it will not move rates far enough. But it is difficult to imagine that under floating rates the inflationary consequences of such lack of perfect foresight in the private market can equal the inflationary pressures generated by the operation of adjustably pegged and heavily managed flexible rates.

Nor is this conclusion altered by the so-called ratchet effect associated with asymmetrical upward and downward flexibility of wages and prices: when an exchange rate falls, prices and wages rise, but when an exchange rate rises, wages and prices do not fall or do not fall as much. Thus, exchange rate movements are said to ratchet up wages and prices. Although such ratchet effects are frequently discussed, it is doubtful that they have accounted for even a tiny fraction of world inflation. In the first place, such asymmetries are relevant only when exchange rate movements are not the result of underlying inflationary pressures—that is, only in the instances in which exchange rate movements are primarily a cause rather than a consequence of past or anticipated price changes.

Second, even when such asymmetries are relevant, their magnitude can easily be exaggerated. While there is certainly little downward flexibility in wages, there is a good deal of downward flexibility in prices, especially in the prices of internationally traded goods. Thus, in practice, it is doubtful that significant asymmetries would operate unless exchange rate changes were maintained long enough to be incorporated into wages.[62] And exchange rate changes maintained that long are unlikely to have been caused by speculative movements that did not reflect the true underlying degree of inflationary pressures. It is necessary also to consider the inflationary impact of the monetary asymmetries produced by speculative capital flows under the par value system. As Otmar Emminger and Leland Yeager indi-

the Exchange-Rate Regime," pp. 346–65 and 370–83 respectively. For general analysis of these issues, see also Andrew Crockett and Morris Goldstein, "Inflation Under Fixed and Flexible Exchange Rates," IMF, *Staff Papers*, vol. 23, no. 3 (November 1976), pp. 509–45; and Sweeney and Willett, "Analyzing the Inflationary Impact."

[62] For further discussion of ratchet effects and evidence on the downward flexibility of prices of internationally traded goods, see Sweeney and Willett, "Analyzing the Inflationary Impact."

cate, under the adjustable peg, capital inflows into surplus countries generated additional inflationary pressures for these countries, while the corresponding deficit countries did very little to tighten their domestic monetary conditions.[63] Thus, speculative capital flows under the old par value system tended to ratchet up the overall rate of monetary expansion. Given the large magnitude of such capital flows during the last several years of the adjustable peg system, there can be little question of the quantitative significance of this type of asymmetry.[64]

Another argument that floating rates impede anti-inflation policies, which also relies implicitly on the assumption of asymmetry in the way the market operates, runs along the following lines: in a situation in which a country has been suffering from serious inflationary pressures, the market reacts not just to past inflation but also to expected future inflation rates. But there are lags in the effects of macroeconomic policies on the economy. Thus, even when a sound stabilizing policy is implemented, it will take a good while for its real effects to show up. In the meantime, speculation will have caused an exaggerated depreciation of the exchange rate, forcing up import prices and causing further inflation, and undermining the initial stabilization policy. In other words, in such a situation the stabilization policy is not given time to take hold. The frequently advocated "cure" for this brand of vicious circle is a large international stabilization loan that will allow the country to prop up its currency in the foreign exchange market while its domestic policies are taking hold.

In its extreme form, however, this argument rests upon a very peculiar view of how the market works, which is quite difficult to reconcile with actual international monetary experience. According to this view, the private market is farsighted, but apparently only in one direction. It will incorporate expectations of future high inflation rates into the current level of the exchange rate, but, for some reason or

[63] Otmar Emminger, *Inflation and the International Monetary System* (Washington, D.C.: Per Jacobsson Foundation, International Monetary Fund, 1973), chap. 6.

[64] There is considerable empirical evidence that in actual practice there was a good deal more sterilization of capital inflows under the adjustable peg than is assumed in many analyses. For example, Herring and Morston found almost full sterilization of payments imbalances for West Germany during the 1960s. There can be little question, however, that although the huge payments imbalances of the early 1970s caused much less than a one-for-one increase in monetary expansion in the surplus countries, there still was a significant net expansionary impact on world monetary aggregates. On these questions, see Richard J. Herring and Richard C. Morston, *National Monetary Policies and International Financial Markets* (Amsterdam: North-Holland, 1977), pt. 2, and Willett, "Eurocurrencies," and the references cited there.

another, when a strong domestic stabilization policy is implemented, there is no corresponding immediate strengthening of the spot exchange rate based on anticipations of lower future inflation rates.

A theoretical model of the economy that would behave in this way is easy to construct by using the assumption that expectations of future inflation rates are mechanically extrapolated from past inflation rates; but such an assumption would hardly conform with reality. Although the past behavior of both government policies and inflation rates heavily conditions expectations about the future, this does not generally occur in some simple mechanical way.[65] Even a cursory following of foreign exchange market developments reveals how closely exchange rate expectations are associated with expectations about such key factors as the macroeconomic policies that governments will adopt and how well these policies will be adhered to.

Exchange market participants explain many episodes of a strengthening or a weakening of a currency as primarily reflecting changed expectations about the course of national budget or monetary policies, and government policies can undoubtedly influence expectations immediately. If a *credible* stabilization program is implemented, there need not be long lags in its effects on confidence and exchange rates. It is difficult to point to a single instance of a really strong domestic stabilization program that has had its effects undercut by overly pessimistic speculation.

On the other hand, government announcements of stabilization objectives frequently do fail to influence private expectations, which is hardly surprising in the light of how often such announced targets are not met. In short, the composite of private expectations is neither infinitely malleable in response to announced government targets, nor unalterably based on the mechanical extrapolation of the past statistics. The track record of government anti-inflationary pronouncements has in many instances strained the credibility of such pronouncements. Given their inheritance, current governments must work harder to reestablish confidence and the credibility of stabilization programs. This means that stabilization policies cannot be merely announced; instead, credible steps must be taken toward implementing and maintaining them before the full extent of such policies will be reflected in private expectations and in the exchange markets.

During this process, there can be a useful role for exchange market intervention, but the case for such intervention can easily be exaggerated. The main point is that if really adequate domestic

---

[65] On the effects of government policies in conditioning expectations, see particularly Fellner, *Towards a Reconstruction of Macroeconomics.*

stabilization policies are adopted and their continuation is assured, then little such intervention is likely to be needed; while if such domestic policies are not adopted, then even a huge international stabilization loan will be inadequate. There is little basis to the notion that somehow the operation of a vicious circle under floating rates will undermine the operation of domestic stabilization policies that would otherwise have been adequate.

There are, however, times when international loans can make an important positive contribution to domestic anti-inflationary policies. Private market participants will want more proof of the likely success of new stabilization efforts from a government that has inherited a long string of failures of stabilization efforts than from a government that has a good record with respect to stabilization policies. In such instances, as part of an overall stabilization program, it may be wise for a government to invest some of its resources in temporary support of the exchange value of this currency. And if in fact the stabilization program does look sufficient to international officials, it may be wise for, say, the IMF to loan funds to the country for this purpose. Indeed, given the international reputation of the Fund for financial responsibility, such loans can directly bolster private confidence in national stabilization efforts.

It is very important, however, that such loans not be squandered. The market will follow the track record of IMF loans just as much as national stabilization efforts, and any persistent failure to utilize such loans productively will weaken confidence in the IMF, as well as the national authorities in question. One of the quickest ways to undermine the potential productivity of international stabilization loans would be to use them to attempt to maintain some specific exchange rate target.

Of course, some hold the view that the exchange market behaves in an essentially irrational manner; in particular, that any depreciation of the exchange rate will set off a chain reaction of further depreciation as traders mindlessly extrapolate from the change in the rate today to the change that they expect tomorrow. In this view, official efforts to prevent the exchange rate from depreciating would stabilize expectations, even though huge international debts were piled up in the process.

If indeed expectations in the exchange market were predominantly formed in such a myopic manner, then the arguments for using international stabilization loans to maintain some target level of the exchange rate might make some sense. But it is hard to believe that anyone with any knowledge of how foreign exchange markets work would give credence to such a hypothesis. As was discussed above, the behavior of private participants in foreign exchange markets has not been dominated by destabilizing bandwagon effects. Nor has official intervention to maintain particular exchange rate targets had a predominantly stabilizing influence. To the contrary, the market has learned from experience to be quite suspicious of government efforts to maintain pegged exchange rates. If the market believes that the funds from stabilization loans are being spent in an effort to pursue a specific exchange rate that the market considers untenable, those funds would be dissipated in short order, and to little, if any, effect in aiding domestic stabilization.

The magnitudes of private capital that can flow internationally when an officially pegged exchange rate comes under suspicion are much greater than the limited resources available for official international lending for stabilization purposes. Over the medium term, official efforts to maintain a particular narrow range of exchange rates are much more likely to endanger than enhance the chances of success of domestic stabilization efforts. Both the credibility and the lending power of the IMF and other official international lending sources are too important and scarce to be squandered on ill-conceived efforts by inflationary countries to maintain particular exchange rate targets.

In summary, there are modified versions of the vicious-circle hypothesis that are legitimate theoretical possibilities. There are some types of episodes in which greater inflationary pressures would be generated under freely floating rates than under realistic alternative exchange rate regimes. In actual practice, however, episodes of any great significance are more the exception than the rule. On balance, when our experience under relatively freely floating rates is compared with our experience under adjustably pegged and heavily managed flexible exchange rates, there can be little doubt that the latter facilitate the generation and international transmission of inflationary pressures. This, of course, is not to argue that floating rates are a panacea for the world's inflationary problems. As was clearly recognized in the Rambouillet and Jamaica agreements, no international monetary system can be a substitute for sound domestic economic and financial policies.

Some have expressed concern that a dangerous permanent split may be developing between high- and low-inflation industrial countries that could undermine international economic cooperation and exchange.[66] Such concerns about the adverse consequences of con-

---

[66] See, for example, Lewis, "The Weak Get Weaker."

tinued high rates of inflation in major industrial countries are well taken. What is misplaced are the accompanying arguments that floating rates are the cause of, or have contributed significantly to, this split. As has already been discussed, there is little truth to the arguments that floating rates generate self-perpetuating inflationary circles or that they make it more difficult for inflationary countries to reduce inflation. As compared with realistic alternative types of exchange rate regimes, floating rates on balance give countries greater incentives to reduce inflation and greater ability to do so themselves when others do not. What they do not do is help countries to export the effects of their inflationary policies to their trading partners.

Furthermore, floating rates minimize the harm done to international trade and international economic cooperation by the inflation differentials that do exist. Given the different propensities to inflate exhibited by different countries over the past few years, it seems likely that these countries would have resorted to substantial use of trade controls and other protectionist measures if the old regime of adjustably pegged exchange rates had remained in force. Floating rates do not eliminate the importance of securing greater underlying economic and financial stability in all countries, but they do minimize the adverse consequences for the international economy when countries do not succeed in this endeavor.

The question of the most desirable strategies for official intervention under floating rates is far from resolved, but there has been increased recognition both that few countries are willing to adopt completely freely floating rates and that the disadvantages of very heavy official management of exchange rates can be considerable. One now hears less frequently the views that what is needed to make floating rates work better is much greater official intervention or no official intervention at all. On balance, managed floating must be judged as having been quite successful in terms of meeting the more realistic expectations of their advocates. Under extremely trying circumstances, generalized floating has proven itself to be a sound foundation on which to base the future evolution of the international monetary system.

3

THE JAMAICA REFORMS AND INTERNATIONAL MONETARY PROBLEMS

In substance the agreements on monetary reform reached at Rambouillet and Jamaica accept flexible exchange rates as the basis for our new international monetary system. These agreements are often criticized as being seriously incomplete because they do not include many of the proposals considered in the preceding reform negotiations and published by the Committee of Twenty (C-20) in its *Outline of Reform.*

But such criticisms frequently tend to overlook that these proposals dealt with the requirements for restoring a par value system with convertibility of the dollar in reserve assets as a major control mechanism, and that flexible exchange rates have made many of the reforms discussed in the C-20 exercise unnecessary for a well-functioning international monetary system. The following section offers a brief review of the C-20 negotiations and discusses why ultimately a de facto decision in favor of a loose rather than tightly structured international monetary system was made.

The last sections of this chapter consider how the new loose monetary system based on managed floating makes a substantial improvement over the Bretton Woods system in terms of coping with problems of liquidity and confidence as well as of adjustment. Chapter 4 will discuss issues of international surveillance of the adjustment process and control of beggar-thy-neighbor policies under floating exchange rates.

The C-20 Negotiations: The Choice between a Tight or Loose International Monetary System

By the beginning of the C-20 negotiations in 1972, it was generally understood that it was not feasible to restore the par value system as it had operated in the past. The increasing frequency and magnitude of financial crises under the Bretton Woods adjustable peg system had clearly demonstrated that prompter adjustments in exchange rates were essential to improve the functioning of the international monetary system.

To achieve this in practice the attitudes that had discouraged the prompt use of exchange rate adjustments needed to be revised. Furthermore, if some new type of par value system were adopted, a high degree of international oversight of adjustment actions would be required to reduce the old tendency of countries to delay adjustments to mutual imbalances in hopes that the other party or parties would initiate the necessary adjustments. In other words, economic and financial interdependence had reached the point that a tight system of international coordination and policing of adjustment measures was needed for a system of pegged exchange rates to have any chance of working smoothly.

No system based on par values and convertibility could work without the adoption of an effective exchange rate policy by the United States and the creation of a system of prompter and more symmetrical use of exchange rate adjustments by both surplus and deficit countries. Such a system would require that a great deal of traditional national sovereignty over exchange rate and balance-of-payments policies be ceded to the international community through greater use of objective indicators and determination of adjustment responsibilities combined with provision of a graduated set of implicit and/or explicit penalties and sanctions to be applied to those who failed to carry out these obligations. The U.S. proposals for reserve indicators were an attempt to present the requirements for an effectively functioning system based on restoration of par values and convertibility.[1]

In the U.S. proposals, reserve indicators played the dual role of presumptively allocating adjustment responsibilities and also providing a safety valve or "elasticity," as it was frequently termed during the negotiations, by limiting the extent to which a small number of

---

[1] The basic outline of the U.S. approach to international monetary reform was laid out in Secretary of the Treasury George Shultz's address at the 1972 annual meetings of the Board of Governors of the International Monetary Fund. A much more detailed illustration of the U.S. reserve indicator proposals was represented as an appendix to the 1973 Annual Report of the Council of Economic Advisers. See also *International Monetary Reform, Documents of the Committee of Twenty*; William B. Dale, "The International Monetary Fund and Greater Flexibility of Exchange Rates," in C. Fred Bergsten and William A. Tyler, eds., *Leading Issues in International Economic Policy* (Lexington, Mass.: D.C. Heath, 1973), pp. 3–17; and Robert Solomon, *The International Monetary System 1945–1976* (New York: Harper and Row, 1977).

70

countries with large balance-of-payments surpluses could drain reserve assets from reserve currency countries such as the United States. This elasticity was provided by an upper limit on reserve holdings eligible for conversion.

From the beginning, one of the major sources of disagreement in the negotiations was over how much flexibility of exchange rates was needed to make a new system workable. Many continued to hope that, when added to the greater willingness of countries to make parity adjustments more promptly, only minor increases in the flexibility of institutional arrangements would be sufficient. Such hopes, however, were unrealistic. Indeed, given the vast differences in national rates of inflation that had developed, together with the huge scope for capital to move internationally in anticipation of parity adjustments, it was becoming increasingly doubtful that a system of limited exchange rate flexibility based on crawling pegs could prove workable.

Even if underlying world economic and financial conditions had been sufficiently stable to make a crawling peg system feasible, however, international agreement on such a system of "stable, but adjustable parities" probably could not have been secured. The requirements for an effectively functioning par value convertibility system placed most countries on the horns of a political dilemma. A flexible rate system based on an inconvertible dollar was politically undesirable because it was viewed as smacking of a dollar standard and dollar imperialism.[2] On the other hand, the amount of international coordination of policies and ceding of traditional national sovereignty to the international community that would be required to make a parity system function tolerably well was also very undesirable on political grounds.

The importance of such political factors for the course of the reform discussions cannot be stressed too heavily. For example, such concerns underlay Charles de Gaulle's attack on the "exorbitant privileges" of the dollar. As Boyer de La Giroday has argued, a major objective of many countries in the negotiations of monetary reforms, especially in the first years of the negotiations, was "to restrain the country or countries whose currencies have become international from

---

[2] These concerns with perceived "dollar imperialism" were characteristic of what Harry Johnson has termed the "political-economic," as contrasted with the "economic-scientific," approach to international monetary analysis. This political-economic approach "derives from national and international politics and tends to view the international monetary system as merely one sphere of the contention of national rivalries." Harry G. Johnson, "Political Economy Aspects of International Monetary Reform," *Journal of International Economics*, vol. 2, no. 4 (September 1972), p. 407.

exercising the consequent privileges. This . . . objective is likewise expressed in the search for a symmetry of rights and obligations; to realize this is to see very clearly the essential political nature of that search."[3]

Those taking this political-economic approach to international monetary issues rejected proposals for flexible exchange rates on the grounds that this would imply a politically undesirable "dollar standard." Such political criticisms of floating rates and of the analogous passive balance-of-payments policy for the United States arose from a failure to understand fully the economics of alternative monetary systems. For example, it was widely but incorrectly viewed that the major cause of the "unfair" privileges of the dollar under the Bretton Woods system was the lack of automatic convertibility of dollar accumulations into reserve assets and that a fully inconvertible dollar floating rate system represented the extreme form of such privilege.

Such opposition to a so-called dollar standard failed to distinguish between the economics of a floating rate system and that of a pegged rate system. The system of international obligations to maintain pegged exchange rates combined with an inconvertible dollar clearly would permit U.S. macroeconomic policies to dominate macroeconomic developments in other countries, and it could be equitable only if other countries were given a major say in the determination of U.S. policies. But this conclusion would not carry over if flexible rather than fixed exchange rates were adopted.

The distinction between an effectively inconvertible dollar under a pegged as opposed to a flexible rate system was also overlooked by

---

[3] F. Boyer de La Giroday, *Myths and Reality in the Development of International Monetary Affairs*, Princeton Essays in International Finance, no. 105 (June 1974), p. 8. Issues of symmetry were among the major topics of discussion in the symposium on the international monetary system in the *Journal of International Economics* (September 1974), which contained papers by Bhagwati, Cooper, Fleming, Triffin, Johnson, Kindleberger, and Samuelson. Other important contributions to the symmetry discussions and debates and related issues such as substitution and consolidation mechanisms include William Fellner, "The Dollar's Place in the International System," *Journal of Economic Literature*, vol. 10, no. 3 (September 1972), pp. 735–56; J. Marcus Fleming, *Reflections on the International Monetary Reform*, Princeton Essays in International Finance, no. 107 (December 1974); Peter B. Kenen, "Convertibility and Consolidation: A Survey of Options of Reform," *American Economic Review*, vol. 63, no. 2 (May 1973), pp. 189–98; F. Boyer de La Giroday, *Myths and Reality*; John Williamson, *The Choice of a Pivot for Parities*, Princeton Essays in International Finance, no. 90 (November 1971); and Fred Hirsch, *An SDR Standard: Impetus, Elements, and Impediments*, Princeton Essays in International Finance, no. 99 (June 1973). For an excellent discussion of de Gaulle's foreign economic policies and their relation to his overall foreign policy strategy, see Edward A. Kolodziej, *French International Policy Under de Gaulle and Pompidou: The Politics of Grandeur* (Ithaca: Cornell University Press, 1974).

many of the critics of a passive balance-of-payments policy for the United States, such as was advocated in the late 1960s and early 1970s by a number of economists including Fellner, Haberler, Krause, McKinnon, and myself.[4] Haberler and I, for instance, in arguing for a passive U.S. balance-of-payments policy, explicitly advocated greater exchange rate flexibility in general; and we indicated that for a reserve currency country, the analogue to freely floating for a non-reserve currency was a passive balance-of-payments policy. Likewise, we stressed that a policy of "benign neglect" toward the U.S. balance of payments did not mean a lack of concern with or a refusal to participate in general international monetary reform.

Unfortunately, despite statements to this effect in our initial study and further elaboration in other papers appearing shortly thereafter,[5] many critics insisted upon straw-man mischaracterizations of this approach. For example, in his valuable analysis of the choice of the best control pivot for exchange rate parities, John Williamson argued that neglect would be benign for Americans, but not for America's partners. His presentation was marred by a selective characterization of the benign-neglect position, however, that failed to discuss major elements of our position.[6] Indeed, our proposal received as much or more criticism from U.S. nationals than from our foreign partners, which indicates that it was better balanced than Williamson suggested. Domestic criticism, especially by those who were concerned about the competitiveness of U.S. trade, focused primarily on the fact that a passive U.S. policy would leave to others the choice of the mix of financing versus adjusting to any underlying U.S. payments deficits.

Much of the literature on apportioning balance-of-payments

---

[4] Lawrence B. Krause, "A Passive Balance of Payments Strategy for the United States," *Brookings Papers on Economic Activity*, no. 3 (1970), pp. 339–68; Gottfried Haberler and Thomas D. Willett, *A Strategy for U.S. Balance of Payments Policy* (Washington, D.C.: American Enterprise Institute, 1971); William Fellner, "The Dollar's Place in the International System," *Journal of Economic Literature* (September 1972), pp. 735–56; and Ronald I. McKinnon, *Private and Official International Money*, Princeton Essays in International Finance, no. 74 (April 1969).

[5] See, for example, Gottfried Haberler, "U.S. Balance of Payments Policy and the International Monetary System," American Enterprise Institute Reprint no. 9 (Washington, D.C.: American Enterprise Institute, January 1973), and Thomas D. Willett, "Options for U.S. Balance of Payments Policy and the Future of the International Monetary System."

[6] See John Williamson, *The Choice of a Pivot for Parities*, Princeton Essays in International Finance, no. 90 (November 1971). It should be added that Williamson, while not noting our advocacy of exchange rate flexibility, does conclude his discussion of benign neglect by arguing that greater exchange rate flexibility would reduce the scope for conflicts in the area. See Williamson, op. cit., p. 15.

adjustment responsibilities has stressed the political costs of initiating the necessary measures. Considerably less academic attention has been given to the political costs of forswearing the use of adjustments measures. But concern about political costs to national sovereignty has been a major reason why most countries have not been willing to adopt freely floating exchange rates. It is incorrect to view the adoption of a passive balance-of-payments policy by the U.S. as placing all resulting political costs on others.

As was particularly stressed by McKinnon, from an international standpoint one of the chief benefits of a monetary system based on a passive U.S. balance-of-payments policy was the consequent muting of potential inconsistencies when a large number of national governments had objectives with respect to both their overall balance-of-payments and trade or current account positions. In such a world, a passive U.S. payments policy gave additional freedom to the operation of the system. And because of its large economic size and relatively low dependence on foreign trade, in addition to the key international financial position of the dollar, the United States was clearly the leading candidate to play such a role.

Of course, as McKinnon noted early on, there were limits to the role that a passive U.S. policy could play. Too blatant a mercantilist pursuit of an undervalued currency by one or more major countries could still lead to serious difficulties for the overall operation of the system. Furthermore, as became clear in the late 1960s and early 1970s, there were definite political limits on the range of balance-of-payments and trade positions over which it was feasible on domestic political grounds for the U.S. government to maintain a passive balance-of-payments policy. Such pressures were of course an important factor in the decision of August 1971 to terminate the convertibility of the dollar into reserve assets and to impose a temporary import surcharge.

During the 1972–1974 phase of the negotiations, the United States position was basically one of indifference, or perhaps of mixed mind about the relative merits of the floating rate and a new workable par value system; but it insisted that any return to convertibility by the United States be based upon the implementation of an effective, prompt, and symmetrical international adjustment process. Not surprisingly, given the perceived inequities in the operation of the Bretton Woods system discussed above, the U.S. negotiators focused primarily on the need for tightness in the operation of the adjustment process[7] while favoring a rather looser concept of symmetry with

---

[7] That is, the need for strong international supervision of the adjustment process both to assure that adjustment actions by the United States would not be under-

respect to convertibility. Specifically, the U.S. proposals were based on the free convertibility of the dollar into reserve assets on demand, except when foreign countries' reserve accumulations had risen above internationally specified levels.

The Europeans, on the other hand, were primarily concerned that a new monetary system should have tight provisions for convertibility and looser provisions for attaining symmetry in the adjustment process. Thus, while granting the need for prompter and more symmetrical operation of the adjustment process, European negotiators were reluctant to give up much national sovereignty over the initiation of balance-of-payments adjustment policies, and they indicated support for U.S. reserve indicator proposals only if used in a very weak presumptive form. Conversely, most European negotiators favored very tight arrangements on convertibility in the form of mandatory asset settlement. They wished to avoid the possibility of a continued expansion of reserve currency holdings even if the expansion were genuinely convertible into special drawing rights (SDRs) or gold.

While it can be argued that the United States and/or the Europeans were not completely reasonable in their demands relative to their willingness to make concessions, the two major reasons why reform along the recommendations of the C-20 outline was not achieved were: first, the growing recognition of the basic difficulties of making any type of par value system work well enough to avoid persistent speculative crises in today's world; and second, the unwillingness to relinquish formal national sovereignty to the extent required to give such a system any real chance of working. Meanwhile, experience with floating rates gradually eased many of the fears that floating would cause a breakdown of international financial cooperation and a repeat of the international economic chaos and warfare of the 1930s.

The reluctance of countries to limit formal national sovereignty was further illustrated in the portion of the reform negotiations dealing with reserve assets. While most countries in principle favored

---

mined by offsetting reactions by other countries and that other countries would bear a fair share of the burden of initiating adjustments.

As used in this chapter, the terms *tight* and *loose* refer to the general judgments about the overall degree of stringency of international obligations implied. Note that conceptually a tight system would not necessarily have to contain a great number of detailed rules and regulations or pegged exchange rates. For example, a system of complete free floating under which no official exchange market intervention was allowed would be a tight system by this definition. In practice, however, the serious reform discussions were about tighter systems involving a high degree of exchange rate pegging versus looser systems of managed floating.

a reduction in the role of reserve currencies and enhancement of the SDR, few showed any real desire to convert substantial amounts of their own foreign currency holdings into SDRs or to accept any substantial limitations on their own individual freedom to determine the composition of their portfolio of reserve assets.

As Richard Cooper had predicted,[8] there were many real economic asymmetries in the international monetary system that would make a fully symmetrical international system much more difficult to achieve than many experts and officials had anticipated. These asymmetries, combined with the importance placed by officials on preserving a wide range of at least nominal national sovereignty in their international monetary affairs, led to a collective judgment that a loose system of international monetary relations based on exchange rate flexibility was superior to a tight symmetrical system based on pegged exchange rates, convertibility into reserve assets, and strong international supervision of reserve behavior and the adjustment process.[9] Essentially, it was decided that the perceived costs of instituting a tight symmetrical par value convertibility system was not worth the perceived benefits, and the oil shocks provided a convenient excuse for shifting gears and focusing instead on how best to operate a system based on flexible exchange rates.

Given the need to choose between two politically undesirable alternatives for monetary reform—floating exchange rates or a tight system of international regulation—and in the absence of important forcing events that required a decision, there were strong incentives to drift with the status quo.[10] By 1974 the continuation of a system of floating rates in practice had become acceptable to most countries. Most of the objections to floating rates on technical, economic, and financial grounds had been overcome, and the substantive issues were the degree and form of official management of floating rates. But

[8] Richard N. Cooper, "Eurodollars, Reserve Dollar, and Asymmetries in the International Monetary System," *Journal of International Economics*, vol. 2, no. 4 (September 1972), pp. 325–44.

[9] The importance of taking into account national preferences in designing an international monetary system has been stressed by Aliber. See Robert Z. Aliber, *National Preferences and the Scope for International Monetary Reform*, Princeton Essays in International Finance, no. 101 (November 1973). On the importance of issues of sovereignty in reforming the international monetary system, the former managing director of the IMF, Pierre Paul Schweitzer, has recently written, "... in my experience there is no field where governments at present attach so much importance to sovereignty as the monetary field" ("Political Aspects of Managing the International Monetary System," *International Affairs*, vol. 52, no. 2 [April 1976], p. 208).

[10] In the early part of the negotiations, this tendency was reinforced by the major concern of the European countries with their own intra-European monetary arrangements.

political concerns about formal acceptance of a system of floating rates were not overcome as quickly.[11]

As experience with floating continued, and recognition of the difficulties of trying to run an adjustably pegged system in a world of high capital mobility increased, the expected life span of the floating rate system lengthened. This gradual shift in attitudes and softening of official position over time made it possible at last to reach agreement at Jamaica on the formal legalization of floating rates. Desires for formal symmetry and "protection of past positions," however, dictated the need for ingenious technical compromise in legal language and provisions so that the remaining major disputants, the United States and France, could both claim victories to their constituencies. This is just what had been done with the international liquidity negotiations, where giving the new international reserve instrument the name of Special Drawing Rights allowed both those who had advocated creating a new asset and the French, who had argued that there should only be a new form of credit, to claim to have won a technical victory for their positions.[12]

The new Articles of Agreement legalize floating exchange rates and also provide procedures for a possible future return to a par value system. Thus, there is formal scope for advocates of both fixed and floating rates to claim victory at Rambouillet and Jamaica, although in practice the agreements reflect a substantive consensus among the main industrial countries on the desirability of flexible exchange rates and underlying economic and monetary stability, and recognition that attempts to peg exchange rates cannot by themselves create international monetary stability.

The Jamaica reforms represented a substantial setback to those who saw international coordination of policies and the ceding of

---

[11] As Richard Cooper wrote in 1975, "Formal arrangements induce sovereign states to insist on formal symmetry in status, partly to cater to national sentiment at home. Informal arrangements carry no such compulsion. To the extent that asymmetries of treatment are important for efficient functioning, informal arrangements are therefore likely to be superior to formal arrangements that emerge from a negotiating process.... precisely such informal arrangements seem to mark the current monetary regime of managed flexibility of exchange rates, which few (if any) countries are willing to accept formally but which most (if not all) fully accept in practice" ("Prolegomena to the Choice of an International Monetary System," *International Organization*, vol. 29, no. 1 [Winter 1975], p. 96).

[12] On the SDR negotiations, see Stephen D. Cohen, *International Monetary Reform, 1964–1969: The Political Dimension* (New York: Praeger, 1970); Fritz Machlup, *Remaking the International Monetary System* (Baltimore: Johns Hopkins University Press, 1968); Solomon, *The International Monetary System*; and Susan Strange, *International Monetary Relations* (London: Oxford University Press, 1976).

national authority to international forums as important goals in their own right. But such a view is not the only formulation of internationalist objectives. A substantial body of experience and analysis has accumulated, particularly in connection with economic and monetary integration in Europe, which strongly questions whether the adoption of institutions requiring close coordination of national policies to achieve efficient outcomes really contributes to international cooperation. All too often, attempts in this direction have resulted in increased friction among countries and a decline in international good will and cooperation. It seems a much wiser and more prudent course to recognize differences in national preferences and adopt a system that minimizes conflicts among these preferences than to attempt the other extreme of designing a system that would work nicely if countries would only change their preferences and to hope that the latter will occur.[13]

The Jamaica Agreements took the former course and are likely to have little appeal to utopians—either those who would insist on completely freely floating rates for all countries, or those who would favor complete fixity combined with one or another blueprint for making such a system operate. The agreements do, however, contain the framework of a system that is likely to minimize conflicts among governments as they are. It is a loose rather than a tight system and as such is more difficult to analyze in detail. But then the primary objective in designing an international monetary system is not to make life easy for the analyst.

The Completeness of the Jamaica Agreements

The outcome of the long process of negotiations on international monetary reform which culminated at Jamaica is an agreement on a basic framework and principles within which international monetary relations will evolve through time. The agreements do not purport to be complete in the sense that they offer detailed solutions for issues. But the current array of international monetary relationships as sanctioned by the Jamaica Agreements do represent a substantial improvement over the original Bretton Woods system in terms of all

---

13 Of course, the purpose of almost any set of international discussions or negotiations is to influence preferences and behavior as well as to determine rules. But there is much to be said for designing international institutions and agreements to cope with the imperfect world and national governments as they are, while attempting to nudge and entice countries to move in desirable directions, rather than drawing up blueprints predicated on governments substantially changing their behavior.

three of the major problem areas of the international monetary system—adjustment, liquidity, and confidence. The agreements at Rambouillet and Jamaica have also further strengthened both the formal and informal mechanisms for international monetary discussions and cooperation, thus improving their ability to deal with the continuing flow of issues and problems in the operation of the international monetary system.[14]

Some continue to argue, however, that despite the formal international nature of the Jamaica Agreements, we still do not have a genuine international monetary system, and even that Jamaica has legalized anarchy. To a considerable degree such criticism comes from those who preferred the creation of a tight rather than loose international monetary system as discussed in the preceding section. But as will be argued below, it is not really legitimate to refer only to tight versions as constituting a system. Discussions of what may and may not appropriately be termed an international monetary system have proven to be quite susceptible to semantic gymnastics which generate much more heat than light.[15] The basic difficulty in drawing an analytical distinction between what should and should not be characterized as a system is that in practice no operational system of international monetary relationships will have all ground rules and functional interrelationships fully specified. This was true of real-world experience with the gold standard as well as the more highly structured agreements at Bretton Woods.

Some commentators have also questioned whether it is appropriate to refer to the Jamaica Agreements as a "reform" of the international monetary system. Here the critics are on somewhat stronger semantic grounds in terms of Machlup's definition of reforms as "de-

---

[14] It had become rather commonplace for critics to charge that we did not have an international monetary system, or that we had an international monetary disorder rather than order. In a formal sense, such charges were true from the time of the formal termination of the convertibility of the dollar into gold in August 1971, until the recent Rambouillet and Jamaica agreements. It is understandable that over this period questions were raised by some experts about the legitimacy of the system of floating rates, despite its widespread de facto acceptance. Fortunately, the Jamaica Agreements remove this question of legitimacy from contention.

[15] In reviewing the recent debate, I concluded that if international monetary relationships are viewed unfavorably by the author, they are usually defined as a nonsystem or as monetary disorder, while if they are viewed favorably they are referred to as a system or order. On this score, I must acknowledge my own guilt in my paper on "Options for U.S. Balance of Payments Policy," in U.S., Congress, Subcommittee on International Exchange and Payments of the Joint Economic Committee, *The Balance of Payments Mess*, 92d Congress, 1st session, June 23, 1971, pp. 382–92.

signed changes of the system."[16] As Machlup goes on to argue, "It would be a mistake to think that most of the past changes in the international monetary system have been 'reforms.'"[17] This is true as well of the main feature of the Jamaica Agreements, the widespread adoption of flexible exchange rates as the basis for the international monetary system. The initial moves toward a system of flexible exchange rates did not result from internationally planned reforms, but as responses to the pressure of events.[18] The major significance of the Jamaica Agreements is the official acceptance of floating exchange rates as the basis of a desirable international monetary system over the longer term. To those who wished to see the world moved back away from flexible exchange rates, then the Jamaica Agreements were certainly not a reform. But to advocates of a system based on flexibility of exchange rates, the agreements might be described as the planned recognition of the desirability of changes that had occurred in a largely unplanned way. Such a view is consistent with the cogent arguments made by Peter Kenen several years ago that "the work of the Committee of Twenty and of its successors is not to build a monetary system, but to describe in accurate, enduring terms the system that exists and to accommodate additional change."[19]

Thus, the Jamaica Agreements are not primarily of significance for the structural changes they made, but for fostering the general acceptance of a common set of views (what Under Secretary of the Treasury Edwin Yeo has called a "shared analysis") of the basis of a sound international monetary system. These views included not just the acceptance of flexibility of exchange rates, but also the need for close communication, consultation, and cooperation among the major governments involved, as well as recognition that stability in exchange rates could come only from stability in underlying economic and financial conditions.

As Otmar Emminger, deputy governor of the Deutsche Bundesbank, has recently described this shared analysis, it is based on the consideration that

> . . . greater exchange rate stability cannot in the long run be
> enforced merely by intervention and exchange rate manipu-

---

[16] Fritz Machlup, *International Monetary Systems* (Morristown, N.J.: General Learning Press, 1975), p. 2.

[17] Ibid., p. 2.

[18] For a good discussion on this point, see Michael J. Brenner, *The Politics of International Monetary Reform—The Exchange Crisis* (Cambridge, Mass.: Bollinger Publishing Co., 1976).

[19] Peter B. Kenen, "Reforming the Monetary System—You Can't Get There From Here," *Euromoney* (October 1974), p. 19.

lation since the external stability of a currency must be underpinned by domestic stability. The Rambouillet communiqué states that exchange rate stability "involves efforts to restore greater stability in underlying economic and financial conditions," and similar wording was incorporated in the new Article IV of the IMF Articles of Agreement. There will no longer be an attempt, as in the Bretton Woods system, to impose stable exchange rates from outside by decreeing intervention points and international intervention obligations in the hope that internal economic and fiscal policies will follow suit. Instead, an attempt is to be made to achieve exchange rate stability from within by internal stability and with the help of market forces. This represents a sort of "Copernican revolution" in the approach to exchange rate policy.[20]

Because it is virtually impossibile to devise both sound and detailed procedures for international monetary relationships in a world of rapidly changing circumstances and of nations with a wide diversity of economic and financial characteristics and jealously guarded interests in maintaining a high degree of formal national sovereignty, the codification advocated by Kenen can only be achieved at a rather general level. Thus, the documents that emerged from Jamaica should be viewed more in the spirit of the development of the unwritten constitution of the United Kingdom than the much more highly structured set of procedures specified at Bretton Woods.[21] In effect, the Rambouillet and Jamaica agreements focus primarily on the major principles of acceptable monetary behavior, leaving specific procedures to evolve over time within this basic framework. Nobody would seriously argue that the Jamaica Agreements represent the end of international monetary evolution. But it is unreasonable to expect that there will ever be a complete international monetary reform, no matter how detailed and comprehensive an attempt might be made.[22]

---

[20] Otmar Emminger, *On The Way*, pp. 12–13.

[21] See also Cooper, "Prolegomena," p. 96; and John Williamson, "The Benefits and Costs of an International Monetary Nonsystem," in E. M. Bernstein et al., eds., *Reflections on Jamaica*, Princeton Essays in International Finance, no. 115 (April 1976), p. 55.

[22] As Lawrence Krause has put it: "one lesson of history, however, should not be forgotten: there will never be a final definitive reform of Bretton Woods. As long as the world economy remains dynamic, changes will always be needed in response to new circumstances and new demand" (*Sequel to Bretton Woods* [Washington, D.C.: Brookings Institution, 1971], pp. 31–37).

There seems little doubt that at least some of the criticisms that the Jamaica Agreements do not represent a system derive from the false view that to constitute a system there must or at least ought to be a detailed blueprint of much greater specificity in many areas than was agreed to at Jamaica. There is, however, more than just semantics to some of the concerns that have been expressed about the Jamaica Agreements. Although many academic critics of the Jamaica Agreements do not expect Jamaica to provide an answer to everything, they believe rather that the agreements either fail to deal with an issue of current major importance or deal with it incorrectly. I would be less than honest if I did not admit that I had a few pet schemes of my own that I would have preferred to see enshrined in the agreements or accompanying understandings; but as will be argued in the remaining portions of this study, the Rambouillet and Jamaica agreements give us a system that makes major improvements on its predecessors in all three of what have come to be generally accepted as the major problem areas of the international monetary system—adjustment, liquidity, and confidence.

This completeness of the Jamaica reforms in this sense is not always sufficiently recognized, largely because the Jamaica Agreements contain only a small portion of the international monetary proposals for consideration contained in the *Outline of Reform* published by the Committee of Twenty in June 1974. In comparison with the wide range of proposals presented in the *Outline of Reform*, the Jamaica Agreements can easily give the impression of being only half a reform or less. Hence, it is not surprising that many have characterized Jamaica not as a reform, but as the failure of reform.

What is frequently overlooked is that the C-20 outline of reform proposed to return to a system containing a great deal of at least short-run fixity of exchange rates—that is, a system of stable, but adjustable par values.[23] These efforts to establish a revamped par value system with only limited increases in effective exchange rate flexibility did end in failure, but it is misleading to treat the presence of par values as a necessary condition for a legitimate international monetary system.

Many aspects of the proposals in the *Outline of Reform* are necessary for a well-functioning system only if a general par value system is reestablished. For example, it is frequently forgotten that

---

[23] This is, of course, not to say that all who criticize the Jamaica Agreements as being a nonsystem would have preferred adoption of all of the major proposals of the C-20 *Outline of Reform* including a return to "stable, but adjustable parities." See, for example, the views of John Williamson, "Benefits and Costs," pp. 54–59.

the convertibility of currencies into reserve assets is, in economic terms, a means not an end. Specifically, reserve asset convertibility is a way to influence the adjustment process under pegged exchange rates, in order to limit the amount of payments disequilibrium that one country can export to others under arrangements of joint obligation for the maintenance of exchange rates. All too often in the past, the free convertibility of currencies into one another and into goods and services has been impeded by controls in order to maintain convertibility into reserve assets at pegged exchange rates.[24] It is these types of convertibility that are essential to fostering international trade and investment and the efficient growth of the world economy.

Convertibility into reserve assets is in economic terms only one of many possible ways of apportioning or influencing adjustment responsibilities under systems of pegged exchange rates, and it often has not been a very efficient mechanism for doing so.[25] Indeed, much of the reform negotiations during 1972–1974 involved the search for alternative methods of improving the allocation of adjustment responsibilities under systems of stable but adjustable parities, including novel forms of convertibility and asset settlement.[26] Where countries do not have obligations to at least temporarily maintain pegged exchange rates, then the traditional function of reserve asset convertibility is not required for an efficiently operating international monetary system.[27]

As will be argued in the following section, the adoption of flexible exchange rates substantially improves the workings of the international monetary system not just with respect to balance-of-payments adjustment, but also with respect to confidence and liquidity. It is quite true that floating rates do not completely solve any of these problems in the sense of eliminating any need for national

---

[24] See, for example, Haberler, *Currency Convertibility.*

[25] See, L. H. Officer and T. D. Willett, "Reserve-Asset Preferences and the Confidence Problem in the Crisis Zone," *Quarterly Journal of Economics,* vol. 83, no. 4 (November 1969), pp. 688–95, and "The Interaction of Adjustment and Gold-Conversion Policies in a Reserve Currency System," *Western Economic Journal,* vol. 8, no. 1 (March 1970), pp. 47–60.

[26] For discussion of many of these proposals and the various types of convertibility, see Fellner, "Dollar's Place," and Kenen, "Convertibility and Consolidation."

[27] Tom de Vries has raised with some sense of urgency the question of settlement of claims and debts resulting from official intervention under managed floating. It is difficult to see, however, how this is really a serious international problem under generalized floats. It is an issue for particular countries maintaining pegged or jointly managed floats vis-à-vis each other, but it would seem best to allow each such group of countries to make its own decision in this regard. De Vries, "Jamaica."

or international concern with the operation of the international monetary system. But when realistic comparison is made with the previously existing Bretton Woods arrangements, the new system of flexible exchange rates makes substantial improvements in all three areas.

In this regard I would take strong exception to the implications that might be drawn from Fritz Machlup's recent review of the Jamaica Agreements in which he argues that somewhere between the Committee of Twenty's *Outline of Reform* of June 1974 and the Jamaica Agreement of January 1976, the main principles for a workable system as agreed to by academics and official experts "got lost or were dropped."[28] Machlup notes that agreement on the key issues among academic experts goes back many years[29] and cites favorably the 1974 *Outline of Reform* as embodying the substance of this analysis. However, in criticizing the Jamaica Agreements for having ignored these principles, Machlup does not distinguish clearly between analysis of these principles and problems under a system of flexible exchange rates, on the one hand, and under an adjustably pegged system of exchange rates as was envisioned in the *Outline of Reform*, on the other.[30] While noting that the agreements "include the permissibility of floating exchange rates," Machlup fails to discuss how flexible rates affect what he has identified as the two major problems of the Bretton Woods system—lack of an adjustment mechanism and failure to provide for an effective control of international reserves.[31] Although the Jamaica Agreements system may

[28] Fritz Machlup, "Between Outline and Outcome the Reform Was Lost," in Bernstein et al., eds., *Reflections on Jamaica*, p. 31.

[29] See Fritz Machlup and Burton G. Malkiel, eds., *International Monetary Arrangements: The Problem of Choice* (Princeton, N.J.: Princeton International Finance Section, August 1964). Machlup cites the important report in 1964 of the group of thirty-two academic experts on international monetary reform as an example. This important study delineates the main problems of the Bretton Woods system under the threefold classification of the liquidity, adjustment, and confidence or stability problems, a classification that, as noted above, became widely used in the analysis of international monetary reform.

[30] Machlup adds, "that floating will go on is not questioned: it should be clear to anybody in his senses that under present conditions the world has no other choice. Floating is now the only system which can work without continuously recurrent crises in the exchange markets . . ." (ibid., p. 33).

[31] Ibid., p. 30. It should be added that this was not neglected in the "Report of the Group of Thirty-two." For example, in discussing the problems of international liquidity, the report carefully states that "All members of the Group are agreed on the desirability of reforms designed to provide for a better controlled and steadier growth of international reserves if the present system of (relatively) rigid exchange rates is to be maintained, though some would prefer to replace that system by a system of freely floating exchange rates, which in

not be ideal, it represents a substantial advance over the old one and has to date operated tolerably well if not perfectly on both scores.[32] It is certainly true that the Jamaica Agreements are totally inadequate and incomplete as a basis for an effective international monetary system of adjustably pegged exchange rates. An attempt to activate the provisions in the Jamaica Agreements for restoration of a par value system without further reforms concerning many of the issues addressed in the *Outline of Reform* would be the height of folly and would be inconsistent with the generally accepted analysis of most international monetary experts. But fortunately, at least for the foreseeable future, the par value provisions of the Jamaica Agreements represent symbol rather than substance.

Floating Exchange Rates and International Liquidity and Confidence Problems

Overview: The Triffin Dilemma. By the early 1960s a number of writers such as Robert Triffin and Jacques Rueff had pointed to a basic inconsistency in the Bretton Woods procedures for providing international liquidity.[33] Triffin showed that, given projections that the growth of monetary gold stocks would be far below the growth in official demands for reserves, the Bretton Woods system, if not reformed, would lead to either a shortage of international liquidity or confidence crises.[34] If holdings of reserve currencies expanded to meet the growing demands for official liquidity, the ratio of liquid liabilities of reserve centers to their gold backing would have to continue expanding, inevitably inducing a confidence problem. On the other

---

their opinion would eliminate the problem of international liquidity by providing an automatic mechanism for immediate adjustment of international imbalances" (p. 33).

[32] The explosion of international liquidity resulting from the U.S. payments deficits in 1970–1973 should be attributed to the old system, not the new.

[33] See, for example, Jacques Rueff, "The West is Risking a Credit Collapse," *Fortune*, vol. 62, no. 7 (July 1961), pp. 126–27, and Robert Triffin, *Gold and the Dollar Crisis* (New Haven: Yale University Press, 1959).

[34] At the time of the Bretton Woods agreements, it had been projected that gold production would be sufficient to meet increased demands for international reserves as the world economy expanded. These projections, however, failed to foresee the rapid rate of world inflation in the early postwar period. This inflation greatly reduced both the real value of the nominal level of gold stocks and the incentives for gold production. Gold production consequently accounted for only a small proportion of the increase in international reserves during the postwar period. Demands for increased reserves had to be met primarily by increased holdings of reserve currencies. See Eckes, *A Search for Solvency*, p. 94.

hand, if this problem were avoided by allowing official currency holdings to grow only in line with their gold backing, a shortage of international liquidity would develop. Thus, in the absence of reform, the system would eventually run into either a confidence or a liquidity crisis; this came to be called the Triffin dilemma.

This section will analyze how the adoption of floating exchange rates presents a solution to the Triffin dilemma that substantially improves the operation of the international monetary system, in contrast with the Bretton Woods arrangements even as supplemented by the amendment creating a new reserve asset, the SDR. It concludes by considering whether the large quantity of dollars accumulated abroad during the operation of the Bretton Woods system represents a significant threat to the stability of our new floating rate system and requires the creation of some new institutional mechanism for dealing with this dollar overhang.

The Floating Rate Solution to the Triffin Dilemma. As recognition of the Triffin dilemma spread among international monetary officials, informal and then formal negotiations for international monetary reform were undertaken. By the time this round of international monetary negotiations had been completed and the new reserve had been created, the international monetary system had moved well past the ratio of dollars outstanding to gold backing that was to have engendered a confidence crisis and collapse of the system. And only two years after this major international monetary reform, the formal convertibility of the dollar into gold was terminated, thereby precipitating an era of greatly expanded use of floating exchange rates.

Where did the reform which focused only on providing a new reserve asset go wrong? One major problem was that the emphasis on expanding international liquidity and financing balance-of-payments deficits contributed to (and reflected) a tendency to downplay the more important question of balance-of-payments adjustment.[35]

---

[35] It should be stressed that this interpretation does not imply that Triffin himself was unaware of the importance of the adjustment process, or that he thought that SDRs by themselves would solve this dilemma. Indeed, Triffin and numerous other leading international financial experts, such as E. M. Bernstein and Fritz Machlup, showed why the addition of SDRs alone would not solve the confidence problem resulting from the coexistence of multiple reserve assets with pegged rates of exchange among them, and they offered various proposals for new institutional arrangements to deal with this problem. For instance, they recommended that a new facility be created to convert all existing reserve assets into SDRs, or that all reserve assets be used in fixed proportions. See, for example, Edward M. Bernstein, "The Gold Crisis and the New Gold Standard," *Quarterly Review and Investment Survey* (New York: Model, Roland and Co., first-half 1968), pp. 1–12, reprinted in Officer and Willett, *The International*

The liquidity problem may have been given priority at least in part because chances for securing international actions looked strongest in this area. But it looked easier to get international agreement for liquidity policies precisely because the latter were only indirectly related to the problem of balance-of-payments adjustment—the problem which is most crucial to the sound functioning of the international monetary system.

Of course, the provision of international liquidity is not entirely unrelated to the efficiency of the adjustment process. In the mid and later 1960s a greater understanding developed of the residual role that the U.S. balance of payments played in the international payments system. It became recognized that the U.S. official settlements deficit was at least in part a reflection of foreign official demand for dollars generated by insufficient growth of alternative forms of international reserves.[36] It seemed to follow that the U.S. balance of payments could be improved by more rapid creation of alternative forms of international liquidity. Creation of the SDR would help with the adjustment process, not just the financing, of the U.S. payments deficit.[37]

But this assumption that correction of the measured U.S. balance of payments was the objective of the game was based in large part on the early analyses of the confidence problem by Triffin and others, which concluded that a system based on continuing U.S. deficits would be inherently unstable. As was shown in two papers by Lawrence Officer and myself, however, the early formalizations of Triffin's analysis overstated the likelihood of the Triffin dilemma actually leading to a collapse of the arrangements for gold convertibility of the dollar.[38] They overlooked the strong stabilizing effect of the

---

Monetary System, pp. 151–67; Machlup, *Remaking the International Monetary System*; and Triffin, *Our International Monetary System*, pt. 2.

[36] The classic contribution on this subject was Emile Despres, Charles P. Kindleberger, and Walter S. Salant, "The Dollar and World Liquidity—A Minority View," *The Economist* (February 5, 1966), pp. 526–29, reprinted in Officer and Willett, *The International Monetary System*, pp. 41–52. Subsequent discussion on this issue was frequently marred by a failure to distinguish between the proposition that a measured U.S. deficit could sometimes or even usually represent a genuine foreign demand for dollars, which was not evidence of a real disequilibrium, and the stronger and undoubtedly false hypothesis that this necessarily was true of all foreign dollar accumulations and hence that there could never be a real disequilibrium.

[37] A good discussion of this point is given in Walter Salant, "International Reserves and Payments Adjustment," *Banca Nazionale del Lavoro Quarterly Review*, no. 90 (September 1969), pp. 281–308.

[38] See Officer and Willett, "Reserve-Asset Preferences and the Confidence Problem in the Crisis Zone," and "The Interaction of Adjustment and Gold Conversion Policies in a Reserve Currency System." The first formalization of

interdependence among the key official participants in the international monetary system and their feeling of having a stake in the preservation of the system. These factors combined to explain the reluctance of major official dollar holders to ask for gold conversions, especially after the announcement of systematic French gold conversions by Charles de Gaulle in 1965 increased the risk that large gold conversions by other countries would produce a collapse in the formal arrangements of the system. The refusal of other major official dollar holders to risk the possible consequences of demanding gold for dollars just to gain a more desired portfolio composition created the de facto inconvertibility of the dollar for large transactions.[39]

Our analysis suggested somewhat ironically that the system became more, rather than less, stable as it passed further into the "crisis zone," in which the United States had more outstanding official liquid dollar liabilities than it did gold backing for these liabilities. We concluded that the United States could probably go on running balance-of-payments deficits indefinitely without seriously endangering the stability of the system, as long as these deficits did not substantially exceed the growth in desired foreign official holdings of dollars. Our analysis placed emphasis on the role of the adjustment process and suggested that the major threat to the stability of the formal Bretton Woods arrangements would come not from the incentives for switches in portfolio composition as stressed by analogies with Gresham's Law, but through large payments imbalances that would increase incentives for recipient countries to use gold conversions as the ultimate signal of their dissatisfaction with

---

Triffin's analysis was presented by Peter B. Kenen, "International Liquidity and the Balance of Payments of a Reserve-Currency Country," *Quarterly Journal of Economics*, vol. 74, no. 4 (November 1960), pp. 572–86. Subsequent analysis includes Fred Hirsch, "SDR's and the Working of the Gold Exchange Standard," IMF, *Staff Papers*, vol. 18, no. 2 (July 1971), pp. 221–53; Harry G. Johnson, "Theoretical Problems of the International Monetary System," *Pakistani Development Review*, vol. 7, no. 1 (Spring 1967), pp. 1–28; John Makin, "The Composition of International Reserve Holdings," *American Economic Review*, vol. 61, no. 5 (December 1971), pp. 818–32, Makin, "On the Success of the Reserve Currency System in the Crisis Zone," *Journal of International Economics*, vol. 2, no. 2 (May 1972), pp. 77–85, and his "The Problem of Co-Existence of SDR's and a Reserve Currency," *Journal of Money, Credit and Banking*, vol. 4, no. 3 (August 1972), pp. 509–28; Robert Mundell, "The Crisis Problem," in R. A. Mundell and A. K. Swoboda, eds., *Monetary Problems of the International Economy* (Chicago: University of Chicago Press, 1969); Jurg Niehans, "The Flexibility of the Gold Exchange Standard and Its Limits," in Johnson and Swoboda, eds., *The Economics of Common Currencies*, pp. 46–64; and L. H. Officer, "Reserve Asset Preferences in the Crisis Zone, 1958–67," *Journal of Money, Credit and Banking*, vol. 6, no. 2 (May 1974), pp. 191–211.

[39] The dollar remained fully convertible into gold for transactions by smaller official dollar holders until the formal termination of convertibility in 1971.

the size of the U.S. payments deficit. A U.S. deficit merely reflecting foreign demands for reserves and balance-of-payments surpluses was not a real disequilibrium and therefore not a source of concern, at least on economic grounds. When developments in the U.S. economy generated an outflow of dollars on the supply side, however, large unwanted dollar accumulations occurred and the stability of the system was threatened. Conflict and tension in the international monetary system developed when the U.S. deficit, swollen by domestic inflation resulting from the Vietnam War, substantially exceeded the demand abroad for additional dollar holdings.[40] Liberal creation of SDRs could correct the less serious part of a U.S. deficit, but it could not do anything about the much more important problem of dollar outflows which foreign banks considered autonomous—that is, generated by U.S. activity rather than induced by their desire for reserve accumulations.

The adoption of greater exchange rate flexibility, on the other hand, operated directly on the real problem of the U.S. balance-of-payments deficit, which was the undesired accumulation of dollars. By reducing the cost of adjusting, flexible exchange rates make it easier for countries to avoid accumulating more reserves than desired, and thus reduce the major source of tension in the international monetary system. In practice, not only did the adjustable peg system turn out to be an inefficient basis for the operation of the international adjustment process, but convertibility into reserve assets turned out to be a very inefficient signaling device for the determination of adjustment responsibilities. Flexible exchange rates have offered a substantial improvement on both of these scores.

The adoption of a system of floating exchange rates has also reduced the incentives for reserve holders to switch portfolio frequently. Attempts to maintain a fixed price and free convertibility among reserve assets, without providing mechanisms to assure fixed prices and free convertibility, were bound to create the potential for

---

[40] Of course, considerable opposition to the continued dollar deficits was voiced abroad before this time. This was due largely to political motivations combined with the fact that not all countries' official dollar accumulations were desired. While I do not know of any good quantitative estimates, I would conjecture that at least half of the official dollar accumulations prior to 1969 represented primarily desires for additional reserves rather than undesired dollar accumulations as a result of maintenance of a pegged exchange rate structure. Some analyses also emphasize the role played by the U.S. rate of inflation in the desire or willingness for foreigners to hold dollar balances. See, for example, Harry G. Johnson, "Secular Inflation and the International Monetary System," *Journal of Money, Credit and Banking*, vol. 5, no. 1, pt. 1 (February 1973), and Thomas D. Willett, "Comment on Johnson" in the same issue.

a Gresham's Law type of instability problem.[41] Although recognized strategic interdependence reinforced international financial cooperation among the financial officials of the major countries to limit greatly the adverse consequences of such potential instability for the overall operation of the system, a monetary reform package that did nothing to deal with this problem could hardly be judged reasonable.

The *Outline of Reform* suggested that this problem, at least at the margin, be handled by eliminating multiple reserve assets and replacing them with SDRs through a consolidation and/or substitution facility such as had been proposed by a number of leading international monetary experts including Edward M. Bernstein, Fritz Machlup, and Robert Triffin. The Jamaica Agreements adopted the alternative approach of dropping the international obligation to attempt to maintain temporarily fixed prices among the major reserve assets.

It is sometimes forgotten that Gresham's Law—that bad money drives out good—was based on analysis of systems in which the price was set and maintained between the different kinds of money. When confidence in the ability to maintain the fixed peg is lacking, attempts to do so are the major cause of disruptive capital flows and asset switching; and the simplest solution is to abandon such attempts.[42]

---

[41] Robert Z. Aliber, "Gresham's Law, Asset Preferences, and the Demand for International Reserves," *Quarterly Journal of Economics*, vol. 81, no. 4 (November 1967), pp. 628–38.

[42] It is indicative of the extent to which this simple point has often been overlooked that in his very useful survey, "International Reserves and Liquidity," in Kenen, ed., *International Trade and Finance*, pp. 411–51. Benjamin J. Cohen notes that "instability inherent in a gold exchange standard is the same as that described by the old formula of Gresham's Law ... [and] ... stems directly from the coexistence of several different kinds of reserve assets (gold, dollar, sterling, et cetera) in what is supposed to be a fixed-price relationship to one another" (p. 435), but goes on to argue that "in principle there are three alternative ways to cope with a Gresham's Law problem. One is to adjust the relative supplies of the several assets to correspond to the asset preferences of the holders. The second is to adjust the asset preferences of holders by altering various of the attributes of the several assets (the most important of these attributes being interest income, convertibility risk, and exchange risk). The third is to reduce the total number of assets to a single-money system" (p. 436). He completely fails to note the other logical alternative of unpegging prices. In contrast, this point is recognized by Michael Posner, who begins his discussion of the instability problem in the following way: "One traditional complaint is that a system with multiple reserve assets and freedom of choice in reserve composition will necessarily prove unstable unless the relative prices of the assets are allowed to change in response to market pressures" (Michael Posner, *The World Monetary System: A Manual Reform Program*, Princeton Essays in International Finance, no. 96 [October 1972], p. 11). See also Friedrich von Hayek, *Studies in Philosophy, Politics and Economics* (Chicago: University of Chicago Press, 1967), pp. 315–18.

Changes in either official or private asset preferences under flexible exchange rates can still cause worrisome exchange rate movements, but this problem is of a different order of magnitude than the confidence problem under adjustably pegged rates.

The Dollar Overhang Under Flexible Exchange Rates. It is still sometimes argued, most notably by C. Fred Bergsten, that even under flexible exchange rates the so-called dollar overhang, combined with increased desires for portfolio diversification by foreign monetary authorities, is likely to cause a secular weakness or undervaluation of the dollar.[43] Such concerns have given rise to proposals to create an international substitution account or some method of funding outstanding dollar balances even under floating rates.[44]

The huge foreign official dollar accumulations during the last years of the adjustable peg system raised reasonable questions about whether this accumulation might not have produced a large quantity of essentially undesired official dollar imbalances, and whether such a substantial initial disequilibrium might not seriously hinder operation of the new floating rate system. In practice, however, the economically relevant part of the accumulated dollar overhang turned out to be much smaller than might have been anticipated. The meaningful part of the overhang appears to have been largely liquidated during the very early days of the generalized float, and there is little reason to believe that there is now any remaining genuine dollar overhang that requires special attention. Unfortunately, many discussions of the dollar overhang have not acknowledged this, chiefly because of failure to distinguish clearly among various concepts of the overhang and to recognize the relationships between these concepts and other key aspects of international monetary behavior.

The term *dollar overhang* has frequently been used to describe four different concepts: (1) the total amount of U.S. liquid liabilities to foreigners (both official and private); (2) U.S. liquid liabilities to foreign officials only (the official overhang); (3) foreign-held liquid claims denominated in dollars (U.S. liquid liabilities to foreigners plus foreign holdings of Eurodollars, which again may refer to either total amounts outstanding or only the portion held by foreign of-

---

[43] See C. Fred Bergsten, "New Urgency for International Monetary Reform," *Foreign Policy*, no. 19 (Summer 1975). Bergsten defines over- and under-valuation of the dollar in terms of the international competitive position of the dollar. There are a number of analytic difficulties with such a concept of over- and under-valuation, but that is a subject for another paper.

[44] See, for example, the testimony by Bergsten before the Subcommittee on International Trade, Investment, and Monetary Policy of the House Committee on Banking, Currency, and Housing, 94th Congress, 2d session, June 3, 1976.

ficials); and (4) unwanted dollar holdings (in the hands of foreign official institutions because the various ways of reducing these dollar balances are viewed as being more costly than continuing to hold larger than desired amounts).

It is only in the case of the fourth type of dollar overhang that there is any logical connection between the size of the overhang and international monetary stability. It makes no difference to international financial stability and exchange market pressures on the dollar whether foreign private dollar holdings total $15 billion or $30 billion. There is a tendency to confuse foreign dollar holdings with the general question of international capital mobility. Although such factors as changes in monetary policy and expectations of inflation and consequent exchange rate developments can cause large movements of capital from one country to another with resulting pressures on exchange rates, there is no reason to believe that there is any strong systematic relationship between the secular trend of dollar liabilities at any point in time and the size of potential capital flows into or out of the United States. (Of course, when domestic interest rates are at a cyclical peak and considerable interest-sensitive capital has been attracted, over the near-term future large capital outflows might be more likely than further large inflows, but this would have little to do with the secular strength of the dollar.)

Nor is there any evidence of a secular decline in foreign private demands for dollars in order to diversify into other currencies for portfolio or trade finance reasons. There has been a trend away from the use of the dollar as a currency of denomination for contracts, in favor both of broader use of other national currencies and of composite currency units—that is, baskets of currencies such as the Euro and SDR baskets—but the shifts to date have not been nearly as substantial as many seem to think. For example, the proportion of the Eurocurrency market denominated in dollars appears to have declined only marginally over the past decade, as has the share of dollar-denominated liabilities in estimated total private international liquidity.[45] (The decline in the share of the dollar-denominated international bond issues has been more substantial.[46]) Given the gen-

---

[45] See, for example, Marina Whitman, "The Current and Future Role of the Dollar: How Much Symmetry?" *Brookings Papers on Economic Activity*, no. 3 (1974), pp. 539–83.

[46] It should also be noted that a desire to denominate a higher proportion of transactions in units of one type rather than another need not imply a corresponding shift in the relative importance of international financial centers for either borrowing or lending. Likewise, in terms of exchange value of currencies, the primary consideration is where the oil producers invest their money, not the extent to which they initially receive payment for their oil in a particular cur-

eral growth in demands, a slight shift in preferences away from the dollar would be reflected in a somewhat slower rate of growth for foreign dollar holdings, rather than an absolute reduction in such holdings.

In the same way, there is no necessary systematic relationship between total quantities of official dollar holdings outstanding and pressures on the dollar or on the international monetary system. Increases and decreases in official dollar holdings may be associated with either a strengthening or a weakening of the dollar in the foreign exchange market and may reflect either desires to hold increased amounts of dollar reserves or attempts to reduce the appreciation of the domestic currency. Likewise, official dollar sales can be an autonomous development based on desires to reduce aggregate reserve levels or to diversify the composition of reserves out of dollars, or they can be the result of efforts to reduce the depreciation of the domestic currency.

While under today's system of managed floating there may be considerable short-run fluctuations in official dollar holdings resulting primarily from exchange market intervention policies rather than the operation of official preferences with respect to reserve asset positions, it may be presumed that on average there is a close degree of correspondence between actual and desired official dollar holdings.

Under the adjustable peg system it was possible for foreign governments to accumulate greater quantities of dollar holdings than were desired on reserve management grounds, in order to defend the existing structure of exchange rates. But it is probable that even at the height of official dollar accumulations at the end of the adjustable peg system, the genuine overhang of undesired dollars was only a small fraction of total official dollar holdings.

Even in the early days of the C-20 negotiations before the Smithsonian realignment of pegged exchange rates had become unstuck, there was much more foreign official interest in the principle of establishing an international substitution or funding mechanism for accumulated dollar balances than there was an actual desire to be able to exchange large quantities of dollars for SDRs. Likewise, throughout these negotiations, many countries, especially from the developing world, argued against international limitations on official currency holdings.

---

rency. When the role of sterling in making oil payments was reduced, it was feared that this could have a substantial impact on the exchange rate of the pound. Transaction costs in the major foreign exchange markets are minuscule, so there is no reason for the mix of currencies received in payments to be highly correlated with the mix of consequent investment.

This view that the actual amount of undesired official dollar holdings was fairly small is buttressed by the behavior of official dollar holdings after the initiation of generalized floating in 1973 (see table 2). Both the adoption of floating rates and the huge increase in the levels of oil payments gave official dollar holders considerable opportunity to reduce their dollar holdings at little or no cost in terms of other economic and financial objectives. These opportunities notwithstanding, empirical evidence does not suggest a trend out of the dollar by official holders. Although the Western European countries did reduce by several billion dollars the high level of official dollar holdings in New York that had rapidly accumulated in the early 1970s, they had completed such net selling by early 1974.[47] These levels remained roughly unchanged during most of 1974 and then began to rise again toward the end of the year. Similarly, the Latin American countries show no secular trend toward reductions in official dollar holdings in New York.

Portfolio diversification by traditional dollar holders has been primarily the result of adjustments in the proportion of reserve increases held in dollars in the United States. It has been a diversification of incremental flows, rather than a major portfolio reallocation leading to a significant reduction in the amount of dollars held by foreign governments. *Incremental diversification*, of course, reduces the rate of increase of dollar accumulations from what it would otherwise have been, but many would view this as a healthy correction of the tendency toward overvaluation of the dollar, rather than as a cause of its undervaluation. And such incremental diversification itself appears to be a relatively modest phenomenon, as is illustrated by the data in table 3.

Some concerns have been expressed that the new major official dollar accumulators, the oil-exporting countries, will hold a much lower proportion of their reserves in dollars than have been held by traditional major dollar holders, thereby originating secular downward pressure on the dollar. Given the high degree of integration between the New York and Eurodollar markets, it has probably not

[47] Bergsten has correctly noted that selling pressure on the dollar cannot be ascertained from looking at total dollar liabilities outstanding, because exchange market sales from one foreigner to another can alter exchange rates without changing the total quantity of foreign dollars held. Heavy selling pressure from foreign official holders should, however, show up in reduced foreign official holdings, and this just has not occurred on a significant scale over the past year. The published data only give foreign official dollar holdings in the United States. It would be possible for total official dollar holdings, including those placed in the Eurodollar market, to behave differently from the published data on holdings in New York. It seems unlikely, however, that data on total official dollar holdings would tell a substantially different story.

Table 2
U.S. LIABILITIES TO
OFFICIAL FOREIGN INSTITUTIONS, 1972–1975
(billions of dollars, amounts outstanding)

	Total	Western Europe[a]
1975 December	80.6	45.7
November	80.2	45.1
October	80.7	45.3
September	78.8	45.8
August	79.9	44.3
July	80.3	44.5
June	80.8	45.5
May	80.0	45.5
April	79.3	45.2
March	79.3	45.9
February	78.7	44.8
January	76.0	43.3
1974 December	76.6	44.2
November	75.2	43.2
October	73.8	43.0
September	72.7	42.7
August	71.1	42.3
July	71.1	43.0
June	70.0	43.2
May	68.2	42.9
April	67.2	42.6
March	65.5	42.8
February	64.1	42.4
January	63.9	43.3
1973 December	66.9	45.7
November	67.4	46.0
October	69.7	47.5
September	69.8	47.1
August	70.5	47.3
July	71.0	47.1
June	70.7	47.0
May	70.9	46.6
April	70.1	45.6
March	71.3	45.2
February	68.5	40.8
January	60.8	34.1
1972 December	61.5	34.2

[a] Includes Bank of International Settlements and European Fund.
Source: *Treasury Bulletin,* Table IFS-3, various issues.

Table 3
INCREASES IN OFFICIAL FOREIGN EXCHANGE HOLDINGS
(billions of SDRs)

	1968	1969	1970	1971	1972	1973	1974	1975
Total increases in official foreign exchange holdings	3.0	0.6	12.4	34.1	20.8	14.9	25.9	6.9
Total increases in dollar denominated foreign exchange holdings[a]	0.8	−0.4	13.3	28.2	17.5	9.6	21.8	8.1
Increases in direct official claims on U.S.	−0.8	−1.5	7.8	27.4	10.0	4.7	8.2	2.5
Increases in identified official holdings of Eurodollars	1.6	1.1	5.5	0.8	7.5	4.9	13.6	5.6
Increases in total identified official holdings of Eurocurrencies	n.a.	n.a.	n.a.	1.5	9.5	6.5	13.8	7.1
Memorandum items:								
Proportion of total increase in official foreign exchange reserves denominated in dollars	.266	−0.666	1.070	0.826	0.841	0.644	0.841	1.173
Proportion of total increase in official foreign exchange reserves held in the United States	.266	−2.5	0.629	0.803	0.481	0.315	0.317	0.362
Percent of total increase in identified official holdings of Eurocurrencies denominated in dollars	n.a.	n.a.	n.a.	0.533	0.789	0.753	0.985	0.789

[a] Figures also contain some claims denominated in local currencies.
Source: International Monetary Fund, *Annual Report, 1975* and *Annual Report, 1976.*

made a great deal of difference on the exchange rate of the dollar whether funds are placed directly in New York or the Eurodollar market.[48] If there does turn out to be secular downward pressure on the dollar in the future associated with oil-related financial flows—and it is not at all clear that this will be the case—it will be because oil-importing nations increase their borrowings from New York and the Eurodollar market combined by a greater amount than the oil-exporting countries decide to invest in the New York and Eurodollar markets combined. Although such a phenomenon, coupled with removal of U.S. capital controls, may have contributed to the decline in the exchange value of the dollar early in 1974, it has not to date been a significant factor that should lead to expectations of a secular decline in the exchange value of the dollar.

Insofar as fears about the dollar overhang are justified, they reflect primarily the possible effects of the international mobility of capital in general, not phenomena uniquely associated with any of the various concepts of the dollar overhang discussed above. To date neither the traditional major official dollar holders nor the newly important OPEC money managers have behaved to any substantial degree in the financially unstable ways that some feared. Nor is it likely that they will suddenly begin to do so in the future.

As was emphasized above, there are strong reasons for the major official actors on the international monetary scene to recognize their interdependence and mutual stake in a well-functioning monetary system. Such factors were not strong enough to achieve satisfactory operation of the adjustment process under the adjustable peg system, but they have easily met the less stringent requirements of inhibiting countries from following major actively destabilizing policies.

Under generalized floating, international financial instability with respect to currency reserve holdings has been the result primarily of countries' intervention policies to meet exchange rate objectives, and not of switches in the composition of reserve holdings. By and large, today the severe confidence problem that originated in the Bretton Woods system has been diluted to the point that it has now become part of the general question of the stability of floating exchange rates. In this regard, official currency holders have been more hesitant to engage in currency switching as a result of changing expectations and portfolio preferences than has the private market. It is certainly true that instabilities in underlying economic and financial policies and conditions can have serious adverse effects on stability and con-

---

[48] See the discussion on this issue in Carl H. Stem et al., eds., *Eurocurrencies and the International Monetary System.*

fidence in the foreign exchange markets, but under floating exchange rates, the official dollar overhang should not be a source of special concern.

International Liquidity Issues under Managed Floating

Overview: The Limited Relevance of World Reserve Aggregates. In a world of completely freely floating exchange rates for all countries there would of course be no problems of official international liquidity.[49] The adoption of permissive managed floating does not completely solve all problems with respect to official international liquidity, but the greater flexibility of exchange rates in our new international monetary system has made an important contribution to reducing such problems.

The combination of the First and Second Amendments to the IMF Articles of Agreement constitute a very significant improvement over the original Bretton Woods system in terms of the supply and control of international liquidity. The creation of SDRs permitted for the first time systematic internationally planned expansion of owned reserves. The adoption of flexible exchange rates takes the further— and in a functional sense, more important—step of offering countries greater protection against excessive international liquidity aris-

---

[49] Discussions of international liquidity usually center on official liquidity, especially on gross international reserves as defined in the IMF *Financial Statistics.* Strictly speaking, however, liquidity normally refers to borrowing power as well, and the huge amount of official borrowing since the oil shocks cannot be ignored in a full treatment of international liquidity. While this section highlights issues of international official liquidity, concerns about uncontrolled international liquidity at times also focus on the Eurodollar and the effects of the mobility of international private capital on world inflation. This has given rise to many suggestions for international regulation of the Eurocurrency market. In two recent analyses of these issues, Richard J. Sweeney and I have concluded that the inflationary impact of the Eurocurrency has been greatly exaggerated in many quarters, as have the desirability and prospective effectiveness of proposals for international regulation and control of the Eurodollar market. See Willett, "The Eurocurrency Market," and Richard J. Sweeney and Thomas D. Willett, "Eurodollars, Petrodollars, and Problems of World Liquidity and Inflation," Carnegie-Rochester Conference Series, vol. 5, supplement to *Journal of Monetary Economics* (1977), pp. 277–310. These papers contain extensive references to the other literature on this subject. International regulation of the Eurocurrency markets, even if feasible, would not be sufficient to remove all of the concerns expressed about the effects of international financing developments on national monetary autonomy. Basically at issue in the Eurocurrency market are the effects of high international capital mobility. The move to exchange rate flexibility has substantially aided the ability of most countries to increase domestic control over their monetary policies. If this is not judged sufficient to give the desired level of national monetary authority, the only practical alternative of any significance would be national capital controls.

ing both from gold production and the balance-of-payments deficits of reserve centers. The improvement in the adjustment mechanism brought about by generalized exchange rate flexibility has given individual countries greater ability to shield themselves from inflationary developments in the world economy. It also has reduced the excessive growth rate of international liquidity generated by underlying payments imbalances of reserve centers and the consequent movement of speculative funds in anticipation of controls and eventual parity adjustments. There can be little question that the adoption of flexible exchange rates has been extremely effective in halting the undesired international liquidity that resulted from the U.S. payments imbalances of the early 1970s.[50]

The arrangements on gold are more controversial because, as many critics have pointed out, they do not completely demonetize gold from international official finance.[51] Apart from the exceedingly complicated question of what would be the optimal economic way of dealing with gold, the alternative of completely demonetizing gold was just not negotiable. Some important countries were not willing to see gold fully demonetized for all official purposes.

Given these attitudes, the extent of demonetizing had to be the result of bargaining and compromise. As is inevitable in such a situation, the outcome fell short of complete demonetization and left considerable ambiguity about future developments with respect to gold. It is always a delicate question in such instances if the "best possible" compromise was reached, and I shall not enter into the game of second-guessing on this issue.

The important point is that the formal role of gold has been diminished, and countries now have effective policy instruments to insulate themselves from the effects of international financial developments with respect to gold. Some have expressed concerns about

---

[50] As Robert Triffin has stressed, the creation of unwanted international official liquidity reached huge proportions in the last years of the pegged rate system. "World reserves increased as much over the three years 1970–72 as they had in all previous years and centuries. Who can doubt that this had something to do with the outbreak of one of the worst world inflations in man's history" (Robert Triffin, "Jamaica: 'Major Revision' or Fiasco?" Bernstein et al., *Reflections*, pp. 45–53). This was clearly a major failure of the liquidity and adjustment provision of the Bretton Woods system. In contrast, as Tom de Vries has noted, since 1973, "... floating has in fact stopped the unwanted liquidity explosion" (de Vries, "Jamaica," pp. 601–2). This is no small contribution.

[51] The Jamaica Agreements ratified the abandonment of the official price of gold and substituted the use of SDRs for all purposes for which gold was originally designated in the Bretton Woods Agreements. In a side agreement, the major industrial countries agreed not to add to their official gold holdings, but the original agreement runs for only two years. For criticisms of the gold provisions of the Jamaica Agreements, see, for example, de Vries, "Jamaica."

inflationary consequences of the new freedom of countries to value their gold stocks at market-related prices, which have been in the range of $100 to $200 per ounce over the past several years in contrast with the old official price of $38 per ounce.

Similar concerns have been expressed about the large increases in the total aggregate of international reserves because of the OPEC surpluses and official borrowings in the international capital markets. The current system is sometimes described as creating reserves on demand and analogies are made to the discredited real bills doctrine in domestic economies with its consequent propensity for generating inflation and financial instability.

As will be argued in the following section, such concerns derive from an oversimplified view of how the international economy works. There is just not the same kind of behavioral relationship between total reserves and inflation at the international level that there is between money supplies and inflation at the national level.[52] At the international level the major concern is with how government policies are affected by the provision of international liquidity and the resulting operation of the adjustment process. This cannot be monitored effectively by focusing primarily on the behavior of the growth of total world reserves, as was clearly indicated in the past two years when almost the entire amount of a very rapid growth in total international reserves was accounted for by the small number of OPEC countries. The behavior of total world reserves cannot sensibly be used as a guide to policy.

The major thesis of this section is that the most effective way to control imbalances of liquidity is by a careful monitoring of the operation of the adjustment process on a country-by-country basis and that this approach is implicit in the Jamaica Agreements. By expanding the conditional lending capacity of the IMF through an increase in quotas and by strengthening the international surveillance of the operation of the adjustment process, as will be discussed below, the Jamaica Agreements have gone a long way toward bringing the problems of international liquidity under more effective control.

Again, the achievements of Jamaica are less impressive in terms of highly structured blueprints of reform. There is no formal mechanism for exerting formal international control over the total of world reserves through asset settlements, such as was proposed in the 1974 C-20 *Outline of Reform*. But it is debatable whether greater mechanical control of the aggregate of world reserves as recommended in the

[52] For discussions of this issue, see John Williamson, "International Liquidity," *Economic Journal*, vol. 83, no. 331 (September 1973), pp. 685–746; and Sweeney and Willett, "Eurodollars," and the references cited in this paper.

proposals of the *Outline of Reform* would have substantially improved the operation of the world economy. Indeed, when combined with the return to an adjustably pegged exchange rate system as envisioned in the 1974 *Outline*, it is extremely doubtful that a system of formal convertibility or automatic asset settlement would have turned out to be feasible in practice.

As compared with the original Bretton Woods system and the proposals of the 1974 C-20 *Outline of Reform*, the Jamaica Agreements take a more realistic approach to international liquidity issues and promise to work better in practice. Of course, improvements may be possible in the formal mechanisms associated with the creation and control of international liquidity, but first priority should be given to making the current arrangements work as well as they can. The best approach to the effective control of international liquidity under managed floating is through the IMF guidelines for floating and international surveillance of the adjustment process, not through schemes for a restoration of convertibility or automatic asset settlement.

False Analogies Between Domestic and International Monetary and Liquidity Theory. Floating exchange rates, by giving countries much greater ability to ward off payments surpluses, significantly reduce the problem of undesired reserve accumulations. But avoidance of undesired reserve accumulations is not a sufficient condition for a well-working monetary system. Too easy access to reserves or international borrowing by one country can allow it to export excessive inflationary pressures to other countries, even though flexible exchange rates can help other countries to shield themselves partially from such inflationary pressures. The continuation of excessive underlying deficits by some countries can still transmit inflationary pressures to other countries through the nonmonetary transmission mechanisms[53] and contribute to international financial instability by postponing needed adjustments for too long. One of the major topics of discussion at the recent IMF meeting in Manila was the need for many countries to begin to alter their mix of financing and adjustment toward less financing and more adjustment.

Many of the recent critics of the current mechanisms for providing international liquidity, however, have suffered from serious deficiencies in their analysis. One of the most common of these is the tendency to think in terms of a world quantity theory of money with respect to the relationships between the total world reserves and

---

[53] These are principally the Keynesian aggregate mechanisms operating through the trade accounts and the direct international price mechanisms. See Sweeney and Willett, "The International Transmission of Inflation."

world inflation.[54] John Williamson has labelled this view the "international quantity theory."[55] Such a view places a high degree of importance on the behavior of aggregate international reserves and deflects attention from the issues of the distribution of total reserves and the operation of the adjustment process. But in discussing the nature of countries' demands for reserves, a number of complexities must be dealt with which are either absent or relatively unimportant when considering aggregate domestic demand-for-money functions.

One of the most important of these is that national governments are much more explicitly concerned with domestic macroeconomic and exchange rate stability than are private individuals and firms. Thus, even though a country's authorities may have higher reserve levels than they desire, they also consider the costs of reducing their reserve positions in terms of their objectives for exchange rate and macroeconomic stability. And even when officials do adjust policies in response to an excess demand or supply of international reserves, these adjustments frequently take the form of exchange rate adjustments or variations in controls, rather than the adjustments in macroeconomic policies necessary for the international quantity theory to hold.

There is also a presumption that profit or economic maximizing incentives have on average much less influence on the behavior of national governments than on private firms and individuals. There is a substantial body of literature on public-choice theory and bureaucratic politics that argues that because of information costs, et cetera, even under a generally well-functioning system of representative democracy, national officials in areas such as international finance and

[54] The usefulness and limitations of various analogies between domestic and international liquidity were considered in a number of papers and discussions at the 1970 IMF Conference on International Reserves, *International Reserves: Needs and Availabilities* (Washington, D.C.: The International Monetary Fund, 1970). See also the recent survey papers by H. G. Grubel, "The Demand for International Reserves: A Critical Review of the Literature," *Journal of Economic Literature*, vol. 9, no. 4 (December 1971), pp. 1148–66; Williamson, "International Liquidity"; Cohen, "International Reserves and Liquidity"; and the papers on international liquidity issues by Robert Slighton and Egon Sohmen at the April 1976 Treasury/AEI conference on exchange rate flexibility. These papers will be forthcoming in the conference volume to be edited by Jacob Dreyer et al., *Flexible Exchange Rates*. For detailed criticisms of the theory and recent empirical studies on the international quantity theory, see Sweeney and Willett, "Eurodollars."

[55] Williamson, "International Liquidity." This view is encountered most frequently, often in implicit form, in popular or policy oriented rather than technical discussions, but there is some advocacy of this position even in the academic literature. For references, see Williamson, ibid., and Sweeney and Willett, "Eurodollars."

national defense are likely to have a good deal of room for discretionary behavior.[56]

In this context it would not be surprising to see the operation of a Galbraithian-type dependence effect that would be consistent with the amended form of Mrs. Machlup's wardrobe theory of the demand for international reserves.[57] For reasons of national power and diplomacy, and their own prestige, national officials might desire higher levels of international reserves and might place more emphasis on avoiding substantial declines in reserve positions than would be suggested by models of optimal reserve policy that focus on aggregate national economic efficiency alone. Contrary to some of the statements in the literature, this type of reserve behavior need not be irrational, or evidence of nonmaximizing behavior. National officials can rationally follow more complex utility functions than are generally treated in formal economic models of the demand for international reserves. Such behavior could impart a substantial ratchet effect to national demands for international reserves. In other words, as reserves accumulate, national officials become accustomed to higher levels of real reserves and their demand function shifts upward.[58]

In a strong version of the wardrobe theory, the "reserve constraint" might ratchet up by the full amount of any accumulation, and national officials would feel themselves under reserve pressure whenever the country went into deficit. Under such circumstances, reserve accumulations are fully and permanently sterilized.

Of course this extreme version of the wardrobe type behavior is unlikely to occur very often. A reserve accumulation that is reversed rather quickly is unlikely to ratchet up the demand for reserves by very much. But a large number of countries, rather than just a few, would be expected to display some elements of wardrobe type behavior, especially given no official constraints on intervention. More rapid reserve increases would therefore be accompanied by a higher

[56] See, for example, E. Tower and Thomas D. Willett, "More on Official Versus Market Financing of Payments Deficits and the 'Optimal Pricing of International Reserves,'" *Kyklos*, vol. 25, no. 3 (1972), pp. 537-52; and R. Amacher, R. D. Tollison, and Thomas D. Willett, "Risk Avoidance and Political Advertising: Neglected Issues in the Literature on Budget Size in a Democracy," in R. Amacher, R. D. Tollison, and Thomas D. Willett, eds., *The Economic Approach to Public Policy* (Ithaca, N.Y.: Cornell University Press, 1976), pp. 405–29, and references cited there to the earlier literature by Buchanan, Downs, et cetera.

[57] See F. Machlup, "The Need for Monetary Reserves," *Banca Nazionale del Lavoro Quarterly Review*, no. 78 (September 1966), pp. 175–222.

[58] This is a point which appears not to have been fully appreciated in the debate about the effects of "reserve sinks" on the long-run inflationary impact of reserve increases which took place at the 1970 IMF Conference on International Reserves. See the analysis on this point in Sweeney and Willett, "Eurodollars."

average world price increase under a given exchange rate regime, but the lags involved would be quite long and variable, the long-run effects would normally be substantially less than proportionate, and the actual distribution of the increases could have major effects on both the time pattern of adjustments and the ultimate price changes.

Likewise, given the widespread use made today of official borrowing, the connection between a country's reserve position and its willingness and ability to run balance-of-payments deficits is also rather loose. The importance of owned reserves as a determinant of a country's overall liquidity position has declined substantially in recent years.

Analogies between domestic and international monetary theory have also given rise to concerns about a system in which reserve creation is demand-determined, as, for instance, in the following argument by Tom de Vries:

> Most important of all, a system in which each country obtains the amount of reserves it prefers through borrowing and exchange rate manipulation, and in which total reserve creation is thus demand-determined, is bound to reinforce the inflationary tendencies in the world. We touch here on a problem that was most thoroughly examined during many decades of the nineteenth century, when national paper money evolved. On the basis of both theoretical analysis and practical experience, the principle of demand-determined growth for the national money supply has been rejected. Indeed, the proposition that the international money supply is also in need of some central regulation is in conformity with the most elementary common sense.[59]

In a similar vein, many concerns have been expressed that much of the recent reserve creation has taken place in ways other than through direct, internationally supervised channels. As was discussed above, the supply-determined generation of reserves through operation of the Bretton Woods system was extremely undesirable.[60] It is much less clear that demand-determined reserve creation through

---

[59] de Vries, "Jamaica," p. 602.

[60] By supply-determined creation is meant the unwanted dollar accumulations resulting from genuine disequilibrium in the U.S. balance of payments. This has been contrasted with the demand-determined part of the U.S. deficit, which represented not balance-of-payments disequilibrium but official foreign desires for dollar accumulations as analyzed by Kindleberger, Despres, and Salant. For discussion making use of this distinction, see Willett, "Options for U.S. Balance of Payments Policy," and Robert Z. Aliber, *Choices for the Dollar* (Washington, D.C.: National Planning Association, 1969).

payments surpluses and official borrowing has been undesirable in general. Nor should these be considered as features only of floating exchange rates.

It must be recognized that such demand-determined reserve creation is quite different from demand-determined expansion in national monetary aggregates as exemplified in the real bills doctrine. The latter is basically a rule for determining the growth of base money, which, as has been shown both in theory and in experience, can easily generate an inflationary spiral and domestic financial instability. But the closest analogy in the international sphere would not be reserve creation through balance-of-payments surplus and official borrowing from private markets, but rather a rule for expanding SDRs at the same rate of growth as the nominal value of world trade. Even here the analogy is not all that close because, as was discussed in the preceding section, international reserve creation will have both less predictable and, on the average, weaker effects on national spending and inflation via the induced reactions of government policies than the effects the expansion of monetary aggregates will have on domestic private sector spending.[61]

Demand-determined reserve creation in the current monetary system entails opportunity costs to the acquirer in terms of running current payments surpluses or borrowing at market rates of interest, which are not present in the government's domestic money creation or expansion of international official fiat money.[62]

Furthermore, the opportunity costs of further official borrowing in private markets will vary with private lenders' assessments of the credit risks involved. This is not to say that such private assessments will always place an opportunity cost on official borrowers that is optimal from the standpoint of the overall operations of the international monetary system. But it does raise doubts about treating the potential for such official borrowings from the private market as automatically representing a major escape valve from international discipline.

Indeed, in terms both of charging economically efficient rates of interest and of forcing borrowers to face up to the long-run international financial consequences of domestic economic and financial exchange rate policies, use of the private market has probably not

---

[61] For further discussion of the real bills doctrine as applied to international reserve creation, see Lance Girton, "SDR Creation and the Real Bills Doctrine," *Southern Economic Journal*, vol. 41, no. 1 (July 1974), pp. 57–61, and Sweeney and Willett, "Analyzing the Inflationary Impact."

[62] In effect, SDR holdings represent automatic credit lines at below-market interest rates, thereby substantially lowering opportunity cost for users who would otherwise borrow from the private market.

given poorer signals and inducements to international borrowers than has their use of the normal channels of official finance.[63] The relevant policy issue, however, is the appropriate use of official financing facilities and their relation to official borrowings from the private market.

The Control of International Liquidity. With respect to use of official multilateral financing facilities, the need would seem to be to increase the role of conditional relative to unconditional IMF lending. In recent years, because of concerns over the recycling of OPEC surpluses and the export shortfall of many developing countries, unconditional lending by the IMF has expanded greatly, primarily through the special oil and compensatory financing facilities. As emphasis shifts to greater adjustment by deficit countries, more use should be made of the normal IMF channels of lending, which are conditional upon the adoption and implementation of realistic adjustment programs.

Likewise, during multilateral surveillance of the adjustment process, attention should be focused not just on direct intervention in the foreign exchange markets but also on policies that result in international borrowing from the private capital markets. Even where the IMF has no direct leverage over a country's financing policies, moral suasion and the prospect of possible future recourse to the IMF could help discourage excessive official borrowings from the private market and the consequent undermining of the operation of the adjustment process.

Furthermore, in practice a large number of the countries that have borrowed heavily from the private market have subsequently secured nonautomatic multilateral official financing. In such instances, borrowing from the private market has not circumvented formal international discipline because official financing supplemented previous private borrowings. Had the previous borrowings from the private market been judged already excessive, further financing from official sources could have been withheld.

Thus, it must be concluded that while it is possible for official borrowings from the private market to escape international discipline, the importance of such possibilities can easily be exaggerated. The caveat should be added, however, that, as was noted above, widespread use of government international borrowing from both private

---

[63] Only in the last few years has the literature on economics begun to recognize adequately the effects of the rate of return on international reserves and official borrowing. Previously, concern had been almost exclusively with quantities. See, for example, Tower and Willett, "More on Official Versus Market Financing," and the work referenced there by Peter Clark, Herbert Grubel, Harry Johnson, and Egon Sohmen.

and official sources in recent years has further undercut the relationships between changes in gross international reserves and the consequent economic policies and world inflation.

In summary, floating rates have brought much greater control over the supply of undesired international liquidity. Charges that there has been a substantial lack of international control over international liquidity are based either upon misunderstandings of the interrelationships between domestic and international monetary and liquidity theory and between official and private financing, or upon judgments that international bodies have been too lenient in providing balance-of-payments financing. The latter is certainly an important question on which there are at present widely divergent views.

It would be most helpful, however, if commentators who hold the latter opinion would identify it as such and, hence, appropriately focus attention on the difficult questions of how much and under what conditions balance-of-payments financing should be provided under various circumstances. Confining themselves to substantively almost meaningless and potentially misleading blanket charges against demand-determined systems of international liquidity creation and pleas for the establishment of better international control over international liquidity does not advance international monetary discussion.[64]

To the extent that reserve creation and balance-of-payments financing may have been excessive since the initiation of generalized floating, they have resulted primarily from deliberate decisions taken in international forums, and not from the access of national governments to private international financial markets or the absence of needed institutional mechanisms. Nor is it all clear that there has been a generally excessive creation of international liquidity in recent years.

It can certainly be argued that it would have been better for some individual countries to have borrowed less and taken greater action to reduce the size of their payments deficits. But given the effects of the increases in the price of oil, it is doubtful that a substantially lower growth rate of overall international official liquidity would have been wise.

---

[64] There is a long tradition of attempts to use international monetary agreements as levers to control the behavior of national monetary and financial authorities and to constrain these authorities to follow policies more in line with the preferences of the commentators in question. The practice of judging international monetary arrangements in terms of the effect they have on "discipline" or inflation per se represents, in fact, attempts by one group of citizens to use international monetary arrangements as a means of making their views carry more weight within the domestic political process. There is a close analogy at the international level with concerns expressed about a perceived lack of control over international liquidity.

Official views of the international liquidity developments in 1974–1975 were justifiably influenced by concern that many countries might react to their larger demands for reserves by resorting to trade restrictions and controls, rather than allowing their exchange rates to float down and/or adopting tighter domestic financial policies. Couple that concern with the fact that virtually all the increases in gross international reserves were accruing to the oil-exporting countries, and it seems quite fortunate that stringent official efforts were not made to limit increases in the growth of measured international reserves. If total reserves had been held constant and the reserve accumulations of the OPEC countries had had to come primarily at the expense of reduction in other countries' reserves, it appears likely that the initial predictions of severe international financial difficulties and widespread beggar-thy-neighbor restrictions on balance of payments might have come true. If there had been substantially less expansion of international reserves after the oil price increases, the result would have been heavy additional costs to the world economy in terms of balance-of-payments restrictions and international financial strains, without necessarily having secured a significant reduction in inflationary pressures.

4

INTERNATIONAL
SURVEILLANCE OF THE
ADJUSTMENT PROCESS
UNDER FLOATING RATES

Introduction: The Oil Shocks and Concerns about Beggar-thy-Neighbor Policies and Sharing the Oil Deficits under Floating Exchange Rates

Some commentators have expressed disappointment that the Rambouillet and Jamaica agreements did not provide for more formal and detailed procedures and guidelines for monitoring the operation of the international adjustment process. Fears are often expressed that greater freedom of exchange rate movements under floating may be used in a beggar-thy-neighbor manner to export serious disequilibrium from one country to its partners by frustrating operation of the adjustment process. Traditionally, given the quasi-mercantilistic flavor of a large portion of international economic relations, most concern has been focused on preventing serious undervaluation of currencies, the overt competitive depreciations of the 1930s, or failure to adjust to the mounting payments surpluses of the 1960s.

The huge increases in oil prices in 1973 and 1974, multiplied these problems. It soon became apparent, however, that an aggregate payments problem for oil-importing countries would not result because oil exporters collectively had no choice but to put the money they earned back into the oil-importing countries in the form of purchases of goods and services and short- and long-term investments.[1] It was also recognized that while floating rates could contribute little, if anything, to reducing the aggregate current imbalance between oil-exporting and oil-importing countries under these circumstances, they

---

[1] This and many of the other oil-related international monetary issues are discussed in Thomas D. Willett, *The Oil Transfer Problems and International Economic Stability*, Princeton Essays in International Finance, no. 113 (December 1975), and references cited there.

could play a major role in minimizing the consequent international financial instabilities and in facilitating adjustment among the oil-importing countries.

Nevertheless, it was feared that despite the absence of an overall aggregate payments problem, serious difficulties would arise from the distribution of payments positions among oil-importing countries. There were concerns that OPEC investments would be placed heavily in just a few oil-importing countries, particularly the United States. This would place almost all of the initial real adjustments on the smaller and poorer oil-importing countries, which could least afford a reduction in their standards of living and rates of economic growth, and which in many cases also were least able to adjust rapidly to major economic change.

A further serious fear was that if the aggregate current account deficits of the oil-importing countries fell on a few major industrial countries, the latter would initiate a scramble of 1930s-type beggar-thy-neighbor policies and would attempt to pass the aggregate current account deficits with oil exporters around from one to another. Indeed, discussions of the distribution of the burden of the oil price increases among oil-importing countries focused as frequently on who would bear the current account deficits as to how the real economic costs were distributed. Numerous proposals were put forward suggesting specific formulas for "allocating" the aggregate current account deficits.[2]

Fortunately, such fears proved greatly exaggerated. Many early estimates or projections greatly overstated the expected magnitudes of total cumulative current account deficits. Likewise, many commentators initially foresaw a much greater concentration in the allocation of OPEC investments by country than actually occurred, and they substantially underestimated the ability of private financial markets to rechannel capital flows. In fact, during 1974 the flow of OPEC funds into the United States was probably more than completely "recycled" out again because of increased foreign borrowing from the United States.[3] Indeed, during the first half of 1974 there was con-

---

[2] For discussions and analysis of such proposals, see Andrew D. Crockett and Duncan Ripley, "Sharing the Oil Deficit," IMF, *Staff Papers*, vol. 12, no. 2 (July 1975), pp. 284–312; Robert Solomon, "The Allocation of 'Oil Deficits,'" *Brookings Papers on Economic Activity*, no. 1 (1975), pp. 61–87; and John Williamson, "The International Financial System," in Edward R. Fried and Charles L. Schultze, eds., *Higher Oil Prices and the World Economy* (Washington, D.C.: Brookings Institution, 1975), pp. 197–225.

[3] Because it is not possible to make a clearcut delineation of oil-related financial flows, precise statistics cannot be given. For example, some portion of the capital outflows from the United States in 1974 was the result of the final ter-

siderable "precycling" which took place as funds were borrowed in the U.S. financial markets in anticipation of making oil payments or financing payments deficits.

Fears of a 1930s-type financial catastrophe resulting from the oil crisis also overlooked the development of a strong fabric of international financial cooperation combined with a greater understanding of economic analysis and of the dangers of undertaking active beggar-thy-neighbor policies. While there were still severe limits on the willingness of countries to take positive actions in response to pressures from the international community, their willingness to refrain from taking active beggar-thy-neighbor policies was substantial.[4] And as was pointed out earlier, the greater concern today with both inflation and employment, combined with the better understanding of macroeconomics, has greatly reduced the perceived advantages of exchange rate manipulation in order to generate domestic employment.

In fact, as events have turned out, the primary problem in the working of the adjustment process since the oil shock is not that countries have tried to adjust too quickly and too much, but rather that many countries have postponed sufficient adjustment measures for too long. Initially, the major concern was how countries could be induced to borrow sufficiently[5] to avoid disruptive and self-defeating attempts to adjust individually more than was collectively feasible. But it has turned out that the aggregate willingness of countries to borrow internationally was much greater than had been anticipated. As a result, in the first several years after the oil shocks only a small part of the aggregate current account deficit of the oil-importing countries fell on the countries in the strongest international financial positions, such as West Germany and the United States. This was not, however, primarily the consequence of efforts by countries like West Germany and the United States to take explicit adjustment actions to achieve trade surpluses, as many had feared by analogy with the

---

mination of the U.S. controls program, but it is difficult to judge how much. Nor does the available econometric work allow more than very rough estimates.

[4] Some would point to the U.S. actions in August 1971 as a counter-example. While many would argue that both the style of the New Economic Policy and the substance of the import surcharge were objectionable, and that concern about domestic employment was a factor in deciding on the New Economic Policy, the U.S. actions were taken in the context of the clear need to remove a large balance-of-payments deficit and thus were not a 1930s type of beggar-thy-neighbor policy. For an analysis of the protectionist elements of the New Economic Policy, see C. Fred Bergsten, "The New Economics and U.S. Foreign Policy," *Foreign Affairs*, vol. 50, no. 2 (January 1972), reprinted in C. Fred Bergsten, *Toward a New International Economic Order: Selected Papers of C. Fred Bergsten, 1972–1974* (Washington, D.C.: Brookings Institution, 1975).

[5] That is, accept net capital inflows and consequent current account deficits.

1930s. Rather, it largely represented the residual effect of many countries hesitating to begin adjustments themselves.

Our success in avoiding the worst of the conceivable outcomes of the oil shocks should not, however, be allowed to lull us into a false sense of security. We have been fortunate that reactions initially took the form of countries being too willing to run payments deficits, rather than too eager to compete for surpluses. But the absence of an aggregate international financial problem associated with the oil-related current account imbalances does not mean that the accumulation by individual countries of economic indebtedness has no consequences for international financial stability. We have reached the point where, to secure a sounder world payments structure, more emphasis must be placed on making greater adjustments by a number of countries that have much larger payments deficits than can be accounted for just by increased oil payments.

The need for a more balanced world payments structure was one of the major items on the agenda at the 1976 IMF annual meeting in Manila. Achieving better balance will require both more adjustments by those countries with excessive deficits, and the willingness of financially strong countries to abstain from policies that would frustrate these attempts.

The achievement of better balance will be greatly facilitated by the informed analysis and discussions that are a part of multilateral surveillance of the adjustment process. The process of multilateral surveillance will take place in a wide variety of forums—bilateral discussions, regional groupings, small groups of heads of state or top financial officials, and the meetings of various organizations like the OECD, et cetera. The IMF retains the prime responsibility for "umpiring" or overseeing the adjustment process.

In such discussions it is important to distinguish between the ex post pattern of current account deficits that occurs, and the way in which this pattern comes about. For example, it is frequently argued that the current account surpluses of West Germany, Japan, and others intensify balance-of-payments pressures on other countries. This is clearly true if such surpluses are the result of active policies designed to acquire or maintain strong current account positions. In such instances the strong countries are impeding the efforts of financially weaker countries to adjust, and it is certainly appropriate to exert pressure on such countries to keep them from undercutting the operation of the international adjustment mechanism.

However, suppose a country permits its current account to be determined by market forces and other countries' adjustment policies. If it still runs a current account surplus, it does not seem clear at all that this should be judged as significantly intensifying the pressures on other countries.

Since the current system is one of less than freely floating rates, it still retains some elements present of the old "who should adjust" problem which existed under Bretton Woods. Thus some encouragement for positive government actions in the strong countries may be a desirable complement to encouragement of countries with excessive deficits to adjust, but this should be clearly distinguished from the much stronger injunction against active policies to thwart other countries' adjustment efforts.

Of course, in practice it will not always be possible to determine when a country is using indirect policy measures to obtain or maintain a strong current account position. But discussions of this issue should be based on an economic perspective rather than on a mechanical focus on current account figures alone. For example if the strengthening of a country's current account position came from an increase in aid flows to developing countries, one certainly would be hard put to argue that this was an antisocial development.

Discussion of Reserve Indicators and International Surveillance during the C-20 Negotiations

The Rambouillet and Jamaica agreements recognized that there were no easy statistical shortcuts to monitoring the operation of the international adjustment process. This does not mean that statistical indicators should not be extensively used in overseeing the operation of the adjustment process or that measures of reserve movements and close substitutes would not be important in determining disequilibrium and manipulation. But even with respect to reserve indicators, it would probably be unwise to attempt to secure international agreement on definite quantitative limitations.

Such a view does not reject the reserve indicator approach proposed by the United States during the C-20 negotiations. Rather, it acknowledges the difficulties of designing any one statistical series that will capture tolerably well the effects of direct government influences on the foreign exchange market. This difficulty is compounded by the tendency of countries, jealous of their formal sovereignty, to be willing to behave more cooperatively in practice than is implied by the specific formal international commitments they are willing to undertake. Thus, even if it were possible to overcome the overwhelming technical problems and construct a good set of reserve indicators, it is doubtful that explicit quantitative limits could be negotiated that

113

would be sufficiently tight to be very useful. Indeed, such an agreement might be counterproductive, as countries would have a stronger defense for manipulative actions if they were still within internationally agreed limits.

For example, since the initiation of generalized floating in 1973, despite widespread unwillingness to accept the U.S. reserve indicator proposals to limit fluctuations in countries' gross reserve levels, there has been in general much less fluctuation in the reserve positions of the industrial countries than would have been allowed under the most stringent versions of the U.S. reserve indicator proposals during the C-20 negotiations. Of course, there have been many other factors at work, such as the move to floating rates and the oil shocks, that make comparison difficult; but the point remains that with the exception of the oil exporting countries, there has been no significant increase in balance-of-payments surpluses and in the associated generation or maintenance of undervalued exchange rates since the end of the par value system.

The main objective criteria that were suggested for use as presumptive rules or guidelines during the C-20 negotiations were spot exchange rates, forward exchange rates, and various reserve and balance-of-payments measures. It soon became apparent that there was no single objective indicator that was satisfactory for all relevant considerations; and indeed, few if any ever had anticipated that there would be a simple magic formula. While it was generally agreed that all these variables should be taken into account in multilateral surveillance, there were seen to be advantages also to using a more formal set of guidelines, "excessive" deviations from which would require justification before representatives of the international community.

Such a view was incorporated in the U.S. proposals to use reserve changes as a major guide to the apportionment of adjustment responsibilities. Under the U.S. proposal, surplus as well as deficit countries could be called on to undertake some form of adjustment response to correct a balance-of-payments disequilibrium. While a number of criteria had been suggested for use as presumptive rules or guidelines, the single most valid indicator of an actual or emerging disequilibrium was believed by the U.S. negotiators to be a persistent movement of a country's reserves in one direction or another from some "normal" level. (The normal level would of course be adjusted over time to account for changing demands for international liquidity as the world economy expanded.) A sizable deviation of a country's reserve position from its norm would signal the need for consultation on whether or not some form of adjustment response might be called for.

Although the U.S. proposal was initially viewed by some as a significant departure from the Bretton Woods system, its origin, in fact, can be traced to Keynes's proposal for taxing excess reserve accumulations and to provisions in the scarce currency clause in the Articles of Agreement.[6] An approach of this sort had also been advocated in several academic studies. In the mid-1960s, for instance, Modigliani and Kenen outlined a proposal establishing reserve targets for countries and applying sanctions against countries whose imbalance fell outside a "normal range."[7] The scheme was envisioned primarily as a means of obtaining agreement about the creation and distribution of international liquidity. Similarly, the Bürgenstock Conference in 1969 discussed a number of proposals that recommended limited forms of exchange rate flexibility and that used a country's official reserve position to determine when adjustment was called for. While these schemes differed according to specific rules that might be applied, each attempted to set limits on the amounts of reserve accumulation or losses that would be allowed before the disequilibrium was deemed a matter of international concern.

While some of the major proposals for automatic or presumptive crawling pegs or sliding parities were geared to reserve movements rather than movements of spot or forward exchange rates, reserve developments had the strong advantage as a presumptive indicator that they could be used over a much longer term. The major problem of coordinating exchange rate and balance-of-payments policies had not been the short-term one of governments intervening at cross-purposes in the foreign exchange markets to actively influence their exchange rates. It was rather that countries had often defended their exchange parities long after they should have let them change, thereby generating large balance-of-payments disequilibriums. This problem could be attacked directly by setting limits on the amounts of reserve accumulation or losses that would be allowed before the disequilibrium was deemed to become a matter of international concern.

One of the basic ideas of the Bretton Woods system was that

---

[6] See, for example, Trevor G. Underwood, "Analysis of Proposals for Using Objective Indicators as a Guide to Exchange Rate Changes," IMF, *Staff Papers*, vol. 20, no. 1 (March 1973), pp. 100–17, and J. Keith Horsefield, "Proposal for Using Objective Indicators as a Guide to Exchange-Rate Changes: A Historical Comment," IMF, *Staff Papers*, vol. 20, no. 3 (November 1973), pp. 832–37.

[7] F. Modigliani and Peter B. Kenen, "A Suggestion for Solving the International Liquidity Problems," *Banca Nazionale del Lavoro Quarterly Review*, no. 76 (March 1966), pp. 3–17.

currency exchange rates were a matter of international concern. However, quite rightly, few if any countries were willing to turn over complete control of their exchange rates to an international body. Exchange rates were too much a matter of national concern for such a delegation of power to be acceptable to states as currently conceived. The problem was to come up with an acceptable compromise between the objectives of national autonomy and the efficiency of international coordination. Phrasing the question in this way suggested that countries should be given authority over their own exchange markets to follow policies as they saw fit, except when substantial disequilibriums occurred. This is the most important case in which a country's national policies have a major negative impact on other countries and on the efficiency of the workings of the international monetary system as a whole.

Thus, as a guide for international action, it might have been better to put into operation the idea that exchange rates are a matter of international concern in the form that balance-of-payments disequilibriums are a matter of international concern. Such an approach recognizes that a country that frequently changed its exchange rate in line with inflation differentials to keep its international payments in balance[8] should be much less a matter of international concern than a country that kept its exchange parity constant in the face of a substantial payments imbalance. This approach would give countries autonomy to run their exchange policies as they saw fit as long as this did not lead to a substantial disequilibrium. Thus, the reserve indicator approach was designed to allow as much national autonomy as possible consistent with a well-functioning international payments system.

In academic discussions and reform negotiations, it was frequently argued that reserve movements were not the best indicator of disequilibrium. Reserve movements might often be quite volatile because of short-term capital movements, et cetera, and might not give a good picture of the long-term trends that help determine that a disequilibrium exists. This argument was frequently made by those who preferred to use a measure of the so-called basic balance, or balance on current and long-term capital accounts. It tended to confuse the issue of the appropriate measure of current payments disequilibrium with the issue of the longer run outlook for balance-of-payments

---

[8] There are, of course, many factors besides inflation differentials which influence the balance of payments. An automatic gearing of changes in the exchange rate to some index of inflation would not be adequate to maintain balance-of-payments equilibrium.

disequilibrium.[9] Reserve movements were judged by the U.S. negotiators to be the best measure of current overall payments imbalance, but it was recognized that current exchange market developments under pegged exchange rates might not give a good indication of what future developments would be and that even large current payments imbalances might not always be good predictors of whether a longer term disequilibrium exists.[10]

Ideally, judgment on whether a substantial disequilibrium exists would be based on knowledge not only of current payments imbalance (reserve change), but also of past and future imbalances; the last, of course, can only be estimated or guessed. When reserve criteria indicate that reserve movements over a period of time have substantially deviated from a country's normal range of reserve levels or targets, the situation should be subjected to an international review, including the best possible forecasts of what future payments developments would be in the absence of a change in policy.

Such forecasts would, of course, look at a whole range of factors such as rates of inflation and economic growth. In some instances, it might be judged that past reserve movements would soon reverse themselves and that no policy action was called for; in other cases, action might be recommended. Ideally, such analysis is what each individual country would do on its own in any event, but experience under the Bretton Woods system indicated that governments tended toward wishful forecasting that imbalances would soon reverse themselves and that problems would go away without the need for policy actions.

Although no single set of data would allow as good a forecast of future balance of payments as a detailed analysis of a broader range of developments, reliance upon the latter as a guide to initiating international review gave too much discretionary power to the group making forecasts of disequilibrium. The use of objective criteria to indicate a presumption of emerging disequilibrium were much more consistent with the principle of keeping as much scope for national discretionary action as was consistent with a well-functioning system. And for this purpose, reserve developments appeared to be the best objective criteria available.

Of course, it was recognized that the transition from national to international control could be made in several stages rather than all

---

[9] See Thomas D. Willett, "Measuring the U.S. Balance of Payments Position," Harvard Institute of Economic Research, Discussion Paper, no. 135 (October 1970).

[10] As will be discussed below, there were important issues involved in the question of how to define reserve movements operationally.

in one jump. For instance, while adjustment might be mandatory beyond a broader range—unless say the Executive Board of the IMF decided that there were unusual circumstances present—violation within a narrower range would require the country in question to begin special consultations with the IMF.

It was also stressed that the existence of a reserve range within which adjustment was not mandatory did not imply that adjustments should only take place when the outer edge of the range was imminent.[11] It was correctly pointed out in the discussions that there would be major deficiencies if this type of reserve indicator system were adopted. Such an approach would undoubtedly have resulted in even greater speculative capital flows than under the unfettered adjustable peg system.

A further point made by Richard Cooper was that, by analogy with control theory as applied to macroeconomic policy, the use of stock as opposed to flow indicators would be an unsatisfactory method of guiding actual adjustment policies.[12] In this regard, flow indicators were expected to be a superior guide to actual exchange rate policies, as, for instance, in the formulation of Cooper's own sliding parity proposal.[13] And indeed, extensive simulations by Peter Kenen supported this conclusion.[14]

The reserve indicator approach put forward in my own proposal[15] and by the U.S. negotiators, however, was not designed to be a guide to national exchange rate policy but rather to designate the bounds within which national authorities would follow their own preferred procedures for balance-of-payments adjustments. Thus, as I have previously argued,[16] it was quite consistent to advocate a

---

[11] Occasionally, however, proposals were made of this type. Indeed, Keynes's proposal for an International Clearing Union appears to have been based in part on an approach of "don't adjust until you reach the end of the reserve band," which contains serious deficiencies.

[12] Richard N. Cooper, "Comment on the Howle-Moore Analysis," *Journal of International Economics*, vol. 1, no. 4 (November 1971), pp. 437–42.

[13] Richard N. Cooper, "Sliding Parities: A Proposal for Presumptive Rules," Halm, ed., *Approaches to Greater Flexibility of Exchange Rates*, pp. 251–60.

[14] Peter B. Kenen, "Floats, Glides, and Indicators," *Journal of International Economics*, vol. 5, no. 2 (May 1975), pp. 107–52. It is difficult to know how much weight to give to this exercise, however, as capital flows were not included in the model.

[15] Thomas D. Willett, "Rules for A Sliding Parity: A Proposal," in Halm, ed., *Approaches to Greater Flexibility of Exchange Rates*, pp. 271–74. I also participated in the further development of reserve indicator proposals by a study group sponsored by the American Society of International Law. See *Long-Term International Monetary Reform* (Washington, D.C.: American Society of International Law, 1972).

[16] Thomas D. Willett, "Presumptive Criteria for Adjustment Responsibilities under Greater Exchange-Rate Flexibility," Harvard Institute of Economic Re-

flow indicator, sliding parity system such as Cooper's for a country's exchange rate policy and a stock indicator for international surveillance of countries' adjustment policies.[17]

As the basis for international presumptive guidelines, the idea of the reserve band, beyond which adjustment would be mandatory, was to induce countries to adjust voluntarily while still within the range. Indeed, the prospect of the generation of private speculation if countries approached the outer limits of their reserve bands too closely was possibly the most effective international enforcement mechanism that could be developed.

The discussions on objective indicators also made clear that countries could disguise changes in their real reserve positions in a wide variety of ways and that even apart from this problem, there were other reserve positions that were of relevance in assessing the operation of the adjustment process. With respect to the former question, variations in controls and formal or informal directives to the banking system in many countries could allow genuine balance-of-payments surpluses or deficits to be disguised in the statistics. Likewise, there were no clearcut answers to how to treat forward commitments by official institutions, long-term institutional borrowing by official and quasi-official institutions, and the accumulation of liabilities to official foreign institutions by reserve currency countries. Furthermore, it was widely recognized even before the huge oil price increases that the governments of oil-exporting countries would be acquiring large accumulations of international financial assets that would require special treatment under a system of reserve indicators. While gross reserve measures turned out to have strong advantages for convertibility of accumulated currency balances into reserve assets, there was no easy solution to the problem of the best measure for monitoring the adjustment process.

Such difficulties did not imply that the reserve indicator approach should be abandoned. Rather they reinforced the realization that for the purpose of international surveillance any set of statistical indicators could only be presumptive, and that a wide variety of factors would need to be taken into account in judging tough cases. Thus even if one particular measure of reserve positions were adopted

---

search, Discussion Paper, no. 140 (November 1970). (This paper was prepared for the American Society of International Law study group cited above.)

[17] The U.S. proposals were also designed to facilitate the operation of a system of convertibility into reserve assets. They contained limits on the amount of accumulated currency reserves that would be convertible into reserve assets— in effect, a limit on reserve asset holding. For this purpose a flow indicator would have been inappropriate. On these points, see also Fleming, *Reflections on the International Monetary Reform.*

for prime emphasis, it would have to be complemented with a variety of other measures as well. In such a manner, the reserve indicator approach begins to merge into the case-history, judgmental approach of assessing disequilibrium with which it had frequently been contrasted at the beginning of the discussions.

Difficulties with the Target Zone and Reference Rate Approaches

The difficulties with negotiating a detailed formal set of reserve indicators hold even more strongly for approaches which attempt to fix international allocations for current account positions or for target zones for exchange rates.[18] If international experts could forecast perfectly and national governments would relinquish all concerns for national sovereignty, these approaches would present a feasible and perhaps even desirable way of assuring the most efficient possible operation of the adjustment process. But in the world as it is, neither national nor international officials can calculate correct patterns of exchanges with any degree of accuracy and durability, much less secure the willingness of national officials to have their exchange rates fixed by international authorities.

Proposals for allocating current account deficits have focused primarily on what the pattern should be and have given less attention to how this would be achieved. As I have argued elsewhere,[19] desires for current account surpluses are largely political phenomena. There is no single economic calculation which can be used even conceptually to determine an optimal allocation of current account positions. The economic criteria that might be relevant are too numerous and complex—even if limited to purely economic factors—to allow a scientific formula for allocation.

Perhaps even more important, proposals for allocating current accounts have seldom considered how an agreed pattern of current

---

[18] In its stronger forms the target zone approach calls for countries to announce a range for their exchange rates and to intervene to move exchange rates toward, or at least keep them from moving away from, this zone. The target zone approach differs from the old par value system with a wide exchange rate band, because it is usually thought of as a trade-weighted or effective rate measure; also, it is a somewhat looser approach, in terms of both the frequency of revision and the degree of willingness to defend the outer limits of the zone. Still, references to the target zone approach as being a backdoor attempt to reestablish a par value system are not entirely groundless. The 1974 IMF guidelines for floating encouraged but did not require countries to establish target zones in consultation with the Fund. There is also a looser type of target zone proposal advanced in Europe by C. J. Oort and others, which treats the limits of the zone as consultation rather than necessarily as intervention points.

[19] Willett, "The Oil Transfer Problem."

accounts would be achieved. The world is just not predictable enough for the kind of precise balance-of-payments forecasts necessary for such approaches to be workable. With perfect foresight and knowledge of economic parameters, the technical problems of implementing such an approach would be trivial. Once current account targets had been determined and underlying economic and financial policies projected, the pattern of exchange rates that would bring about the desired current account pattern could be calculated. Econometric models and estimates exist that in principle would allow such an exercise; but in practice the accuracy of such models and estimates is far less than sufficient to make such an approach viable, as is illustrated by the huge forecast errors frequently made by even the best balance-of-payments models and judgmental forecasts. For example, while the appropriate allocation of current account balances is frequently discussed in terms of at least to the nearest $1 or $2 billion, only one of the twelve annual forecast errors by the OECD for the current accounts balances of the six major industrial countries for the years 1974 and 1975 was less than $2 billion (see table 4). And this was for forecasting only one year in advance. (Many discussions of target zones have envisaged selecting a zone that is expected to hold over several years.) Furthermore, with all of the underlying instabilities in the world economy in recent years, forecast errors have risen dramatically. For 1974 and 1975, the average error of the annual current account projections by the OECD was approximately $6 billion for the six major countries. And as shown in Appendix A, table A-2, the error for the U.S. current account in 1975 was an incredible $19 billion, with an actual surplus of $11.65 billion, as compared with a projected deficit of $7.5 billion. Nor do these results indicate the OECD is a particularly bad forecaster. For example, errors of similar direction and magnitude were made both in internal U.S. Treasury forecasts and in the published forecasts of Morgan Guaranty. Indeed, table A-2 shows that in 1975 the average error for Morgan Guaranty forecasts as published in *World Financial Markets* was almost identical to that of the OECD, although Morgan did hold an edge for 1974.

Such figures raise questions about the ability of international authorities to determine a viable pattern of exchange rates for any significant length of time. As soon as any of the forecasts determining the exchange rates went wrong, as happened often, the target exchange rate pattern would have to be renegotiated. If the target zones were broad enough to take into account the difficulties of estimating correct exchange rates—especially with a time horizon of several years as was frequently specified in such proposals—they

Table 4A

OECD CURRENT ACCOUNT FORECAST ERRORS
(in billions of dollars)

	1974	1975
United States	5.6	19.2
United Kingdom	5.8	2.7
France	5.2	6.5
W. Germany	8.6	2.2
Italy	6.4	5.2
Japan	4.2	0.7
Total	35.8	36.5
Average	6.0	6.1[a]

a *World Financial Markets* does not publish a consistent set of forecasts and actuals for either the current account or the trade balances. Current account estimates are published at various times, but the reader cannot tell if they are consistently reported on a seasonally adjusted customs basis. Given this, a good track record cannot be constructed. Some data found in various issues are presented below. This table was constructed by Craig Larimer.

Table 4B

Morgan Guaranty Current Account Forecast Errors
(in billions of dollars)

	1974			1975		
	Forecast	Actual	Absolute Difference	Forecast	Actual	Absolute Difference
U.S.	−2.000	−2.250	.250	−6.500	11.700	18.200
U.K.	−6.000	−8.750	2.750	−8.500	−3.800	4.700
France	−4.500	−5.500	1.000	−3.500	.300	3.800
W. Germany	−3.500	9.250	12.750	10.000	3.800	6.200
Italy	−5.500	−9.500	4.000	−4.500	− .500	4.000
Japan	−7.000	−4.500	2.500	− .500	− .700	.200
Total			23.250			37.100
Average			3.900			6.200

Sources: Appendix A and *World Financial Markets*, various issues.

would become much too loose to be linked to current account positions. Target zones for exchange rates are decidedly superior to a return to the old par value system. They still rest on undue faith in econometric models, however, and in the ability of international experts to forecast international financial developments and to estimate correct or appropriate exchange rates accurately enough to make such an approach realistic.

To a lesser extent, these difficulties apply to the reference rate proposals for international surveillance of floating rates. As propounded by Ethier and Bloomfield and by Williamson,[20] the reference rate proposal would retain the Bretton Woods idea of parities but reverse the relation of parities to official intervention. The Bretton Woods regime focused on when intervention was required, whereas the reference rate proposal focuses on when intervention is prohibited. Under the Bretton Woods regime, countries were required to intervene to keep exchange rates from moving away from parity by more than a specified amount. The reference rate proposal, on the other hand, prohibits official intervention to sell foreign exchange when exchange rates are below the reference parity or zone, and it prohibits the purchase of foreign exchange when the exchange rates are above the parity zone.

Intervention to move exchange rates toward the reference parity or zone would be allowed but not required. On the assumption that it could be effectively enforced, the advocates of the reference rate proposal make a convincing case for its superiority over the old par value system. It is also much less likely to lead to undesirable intervention and to contribute to international financial instability than would the target zone approach as it was recommended in the 1974 IMF guidelines for floating[21] and by several economists and officials in recent years. The more ambitious target zone approach would require, or at least strongly encourage, that in addition countries intervene to dampen exchange rate movements away from and reinforce movements toward the target zone.

But the reference rate proposal is not completely free of dangers as the basis for international surveillance of the adjustment process. For example, John Williamson sees reference rates not only as safeguarding against antisocial exchange rate manipulation, but also as

---

[20] Wilfred Ethier and Arthur I. Bloomfield, *Managing the Managed Float*, Princeton Essays in International Finance, no. 112 (October 1975), and John H. Williamson, "The Future Exchange-Rate Regime," *Banca Nazionale del Lavoro Quarterly Review*, no. 113 (June 1975), pp. 117–44. See also Williamson, "Benefits and Costs."

While some have likened the looser Oort type of target zone approach to the reference proposal because of the lack of required intervention, the focuses of the two types of proposals are really quite different. The Oort approach still attempts to specify an exchange rate zone which presumably should be defended, while the reference rate proposals focus on when intervention should be prohibited. For further discussion of the content of these proposals, see Samuel I. Katz, ed., *U.S.-European Monetary Relations* (Washington, D.C.: American Enterprise Institute, forthcoming).

[21] For a critical review of the IMF guidelines, see Raymond Mikesell and Henry N. Goldstein, *Rules for a Floating Regime*, Princeton Essays in International Finance, no. 109 (April 1975).

leading to greater stability in the foreign exchange markets by providing a focal point for stabilizing speculation. Such an outcome, however, is crucially dependent both on the behavior of the private exchange market and on the ability of governments to speculate better.

It is difficult to judge conclusively whether official or private speculation has performed better (or less poorly) on balance under the current float, and what is the best role of official intervention in supplementing the private market. But it is fairly clear that the countries where official intervention has been the most effective (or least ineffective) in promoting stability have been those that were not committed to defending particular rate levels for any significant period of time. The reference rate proposal seriously risks generating pressures on financial authorities to defend reference parities or zones. In other words, it may not be possible to establish an officially sanctioned set of reference rates without creating pressures that would, in practice, convert the reference rate scheme into the target zone approach.

Even apart from this major problem, some technical questions must be raised about the advantages claimed for the reference rate approach as compared with other guidelines proposed for floating. For example, Ethier and Bloomfield argue that the reference rate proposal is easier to implement than a reserve indicator approach because it avoids the problem of having to define reserves.[22] But they do not deal adequately with the question of how to define intervention, which, if addressed realistically, is open to almost as many ambiguities as is the meaning of reserves.

Ethier and Bloomfield also argue for superiority of the reference rate over reserve-based proposals on the grounds that

> at a more basic level, the fundamental goal of any proposal is presumably to maintain an approximation to an equilibrium structure of exchange rates. There is, in truth, no such thing as an equilibrium structure of reserve levels. When reserve levels are used to define permissible intervention, they are really serving as proxies for exchange rates, and they need not be very exact proxies.[23]

This is again a misleading formulation. Ethier and Bloomfield appear implicitly to assume that they can know within a fairly close range what equilibrium rates are, but this evades the real problem, that it is difficult to "know" what the equilibrium rate is.

---

[22] Ethier and Bloomfield, *Managing the Managed Float*, p. 19.
[23] Ibid., p. 19.

There is usually no dearth of commentators willing to offer their opinion on the subject, but there will seldom be a wide consensus among experts that the market rate is very far from this equilibrium rate.[24] In practice, the relative accuracy of the pure reserve indicator and reference rate approaches would be expected to vary at times both from country to country and from episode to episode. It is understandable that at times national officials in some countries may want to "take a view" on their exchange rate; by the same token, international officials, in confidential discussions of balance-of-payments financing and surveillance of the adjustment process, may sometimes have a particular range of exchange rates in mind as being appropriate for a particular country at a particular time. But using the reference rate approach in such an informal context is not the same as attempting to determine and keep up to date a full set of internationally sanctioned reference rates.

In other words, the reserve approach assumes that market forces are generally a fairly reliable determinant of equilibrium exchange rates and that the best evidence of substantial disequilibrium is the existence of sizable government influences on the exchange market through official intervention or various types of substitute policies. The reference rate proposal on the other hand assumes that, because of poorly behaved speculation, market exchange rates will frequently diverge significantly from equilibrium rates. In pure form, the reference rate proposals implicitly assume that officials can usually forecast better than the market behaves. One need not naively believe the market is always right in order to have serious qualms about the general accuracy of this assumption. In a choice between a reserve indicator and a reference rate system in pure form, the attractions of the latter are far less than are implied by Ethier and Bloomfield. What is more important, however, is that neither would in fact be a very satisfactory basis for international surveillance of the adjustment process. The thrust of the reserve approach is that in practice disequilibrium exchange rates are more likely to be ascertained by looking at evidence of official intervention to influence rates than by making official forecasts of equilibrium rates.

---

[24] In general, if there is a broad consensus among both private and official experts, this will be reflected in the market rate. As noted in chapter 2, conceptually it is possible that where the supply of speculative funds is highly limited—that is, where the speculative schedule has little elasticity—the market rate could differ significantly from the view of a vast majority of experts. This may have occurred at times in the early days of floating, as the market was becoming accustomed to the new arrangements, but there is little evidence that this is a frequent phenomenon today, however. In general, now the opinions of experts that an exchange rate is substantially above or below equilibrium is balanced by the opinions of other experts with opposing views.

By indicating that official intervention should be used to oppose large rapid movements in exchange rates, the 1974 IMF guidelines for floating implicitly endorsed the view that any rapid change in an exchange rate must be presumptive evidence of the existence of destabilizing speculations. As was discussed in chapter 2, however, such a presumption is quite questionable. Concern with avoiding disorderly markets should not be formulated in terms of monitoring the variance of countries' exchange rates.

The avoidance of disorderly foreign exchange market conditions involves both positive and negative obligations. Most commonly discussed is the positive obligation to intervene to make a market where, for some reason, the functioning of the private market has become disorderly and normal transactions cannot be carried out or can be accomplished only with extraordinary difficulty. The emergence of such disorderly market conditions requires a judgmental determination and cannot be reasonably indicated by the use of objective statistical indicators alone. It is also generally a fairly short-lived phenomenon. Thus, in practice, except perhaps for the possibility of after-the-fact reviews of episodes, international surveillance of countries' obligations on this score must rest upon the network of frequent communication and consultation among the finance ministers and central banks of the major countries.

A second obligation, perhaps even more judgmental than the first, is to refrain from official actions that are likely to generate disorderly conditions in the private market. The most clearcut example of such actions is official intervention to maintain an unrealistic market rate. Since such actions have frequently generated disorderly market conditions, the obligation of combating disorderly market conditions may sometimes call for less, rather than more, official intervention.

Securing Effective International Financial Cooperation: The Need for a Case-History Approach to Multilateral Surveillance

Attempts to move back to the par value system by establishing target zones for exchange rates would give us a monetary system that looked much more tidy and orderly on paper, but in practice such an approach could easily create disorder. The Rambouillet and Jamaica agreements did not attempt to construct a detailed blueprint and focused instead on strengthening international consultation and surveillance as the framework overseeing the adjustment process.

This approach is quite different from that adopted at Bretton

Woods, but for good reasons. We are at a stage in the evolution of the international monetary system where most countries are much more willing in practice to cooperate internationally and to avoid uncooperative actions than they are willing to cede specific authority to organs of the international community to control such behavior. As compared with the relatively structured par value system of Bretton Woods, today's system of flexible exchange rates gives countries greater latitude to follow blatant beggar-thy-neighbor policies if they abandon the spirit of their international commitments, but it also makes it easier for them to follow cooperative policies that minimize conflicts over balance-of-payments adjustment. In the light of this characterization, the bias contained in the Bretton Woods system against taking adjustment actions would have been preferable during the 1930s, given the tendencies of national government behavior at that time.[25] Likewise, it may have been prudent to opt for Bretton Woods type of procedures in the early postwar period, because fears of a repetition of the 1930s were widespread. As the system has evolved, however, there is today a much stronger fabric of international financial cooperation and much less danger of blatant beggar-thy-neighbor policies. Thus, the relative desirability of these two types of systems has been reversed.

As has been discussed earlier, over the past decade a greater threat to international financial stability has been the difficulty of securing sufficient positive adjustment actions under the adjustable peg system. Today floating rates are likely to have a much more favorable impact on effective international financial cooperation than would attempts to reinstate the adjustable par value system of Bretton Woods. It is doubtful that today a system of flexible exchange rates needs more international rules to function well than would the Bretton Woods adjustable peg system.[26]

Similarly, at this stage in the evolution of international financial cooperation, countries in general are more likely to modify somewhat inconsistent targets with respect to the structures of their balance of payments—for example, individual targets for trade or current ac-

[25] It should be noted that the Bretton Woods system comprised the full set of procedures for international control of exchange rate adjustments, not just the adjustable par value system. Indeed, as was previously noted, most major exchange rates were adjustably pegged, not floating, during the period of competitive depreciation in the 1930s.

[26] Thus, I would strongly disagree with the assertion by Andrew Shonfield that "It had become apparent that the system of managed floating exchange rates required more, rather than fewer, internationally agreed rules than the old regime of fixed parities" (Andrew Shonfield, ed., *International Economic Relations of the Western World 1959–1971* [New York: Oxford University Press, 1976], vol. 2, p. 7).

count surpluses which are not collectively feasible—on the basis of quiet discussion among national and international financial officials, than they would be to accept and follow a highly detailed set of guidelines promulgated by an international body. On such issues, national officials seem much more likely to modify positions if it appears that they were not pressured into it. There is to some degree an analogy here to the proven need to make international agreements sound sufficiently ambiguous so that all major parties can claim a measure of victory.

In summary, fears that the Jamaica Agreements are seriously deficient because they do not provide detailed rules for exchange rate behavior are understandable, but are not well founded. They both overstate the dangers of competitive depreciation under a system of managed floating and underestimate the difficulties of achieving formal versus informal adherence to principles of international good behavior.[27] The Jamaica Agreements have recommended that the IMF develop specific principles for the international surveillance of the adjustment process in the form of a codification over time from the case histories of judgments on particular circumstances; that is, through a process of the development of precedents over time. Some actions would clearly be deemed manipulative or beggar-thy-neighbor, and others definitely would not. But there is a wide gray area of actions that cannot easily be labelled one or the other a priori. These will have to be settled by multilateral judgments on a case-by-case basis as they occur, thereby achieving greater clarification as the gray area is gradually narrowed.[28]

With so many conceivable gray-area cases and our limited state of knowledge, it would be unwise to attempt to secure precise international agreement ahead of time on all possible types of cases. These considerations are reinforced when it is recognized that in practice

---

[27] Likewise, in practice there have not been serious problems of different national authorities intervening at cross-purposes and generating inconsistent cross-rates, possibilities that have been quite frequently discussed in the academic literature. From the standpoint of the United States, it would be desirable to reach an agreement on the conditions under which countries intervene in each other's currencies; for instance, to reduce fluctuations in the exchange value of the dollar caused by the use of dollar interventions to maintain exchange relationships within the European snake. Such dollar interventions have not caused major disruptions in the U.S. foreign exchange market, however, and the prospects for any general international agreement on this subject in the near future are not bright.

[28] For further discussions of the need to rely heavily on this type of approach, see the comments by Richard Cooper and Robert Roosa in E. M. Bernstein et al., eds., *Reflections on Jamaica*; and Sam Y. Cross, Marina Whitman, and Thomas D. Willett, "Principles for International Financial Cooperation," in Dreyer, Haberler, and Willett, eds., *Exchange Rate Flexibility*.

the seriousness of the consequences of a particular policy action, and even whether it is on balance desirable or undesirable, may be crucially dependent on the surrounding circumstances.

Furthermore, it must be remembered that the ability of the international community to influence and penalize nations' behavior is not unlimited. Attempts to enforce prohibitions on too many minor abuses could well undercut the ability of the international community to discourage major abuses effectively. Too detailed a list of do's and don't's would court the danger of undermining the effectiveness of international surveillance. The development of a good set of specific principles is too important to attempt to accomplish it in haste.

The absence of a long list of international guidelines or regulations must not be taken as failure to recognize the importance of fostering cooperation and discouraging manipulative exchange rate and balance-of-payments policies. Nor must the fact that there are many cases which cannot be evaluated unambiguously keep us from focusing on cases that are less ambiguous. In almost all countries there are pressures for protectionist trade and exchange rate policies which must be continually fought. Important weapons in this fight are both the formal mechanisms for international surveillance through the IMF and other international organizations and frequent informal contact among top officials of national governments. This reduces the propensity in national government decision making to slight international obligations and considerations when the latter conflict with domestic protectionist pressures. The battle fought in the Bretton Woods negotiations by a liberal economic order to keep nationalist protectionist pressures in check was quite respectable, on balance. It would be extremely dangerous to rest on past laurels.

A Final Point: The Need for Greater Recognition That Trade Surpluses Are Not Required for Economic Prosperity

In this regard, one of the most important needs is to secure greater recognition in many countries that domestic economic prosperity is not dependent on achieving trade or current account surpluses. As was discussed above, we escaped the initial destructive scramble for mutually unachievable trade balance surpluses that many had feared would follow in the wake of the oil shock. But we are now facing a second-round challenge. Many countries have overborrowed in the past several years and must take adjustment actions to reduce their deficits. For these countries to achieve the needed adjustments, however, the countries that are financially strong, such as West Germany, Japan, and the United States, must not frustrate the adjustment process by taking manipulative actions to prevent reductions in their own trade and current account surpluses.

Nor do even the narrow national self-interests of the strong countries really call for attempts to preserve trade surpluses. Unfortunately, the desirability of having a surplus in a country's balance of trade or current account is viewed by many as axiomatic, in the same category as motherhood and apple pie. Such views are frequently little more than a generalization of the notion that whatever the account in question—be it a personal budget, the national budget, or the balance of payments—a surplus is to be sought and a deficit avoided. Lurking at a slightly deeper level of thought is often found some modern version of mercantilist misconceptions that a trade surplus is necessary to achieve objectives of national power and prestige.

More rational arguments for trade balance surpluses are based on considerations of maintaining domestic employment and achieving a sustainable overall equilibrium in a country's balance of payments. As will be argued below, however, such considerations are only relevant in particular circumstances and do not represent logical reasons for always seeking to achieve a trade or current account surplus. This has been reinforced in recent years by the elevation of price stability to a major policy objective, combined with recognition of the beneficial role of imports in increasing the overall availability of goods and services for domestic consumption and investment and consequently reducing domestic inflation. In present circumstances, it can be argued that a current account deficit for the United States would also be desirable from the standpoint of having a greater portion of the aggregate current account deficits of oil-importing countries fall on countries with the soundest international financial positions.

The U.S. announcement in 1971 of specific objectives with respect to improvement in its current account position was not presented in terms of some general view that a U.S. trade surplus was necessary or desirable per se. Rather, it was based on estimates of what would be required of the trade and current accounts to achieve a sustainable overall balance-of-payments equilibrium under a new set of fixed exchange rate relationships, given the outlook for other components of the balance of payments. In other words, they were presented as a proximate target of policy in a particular set of circumstances, not as an ultimate objective of policy for its own sake. The emergence of a new international monetary system based on flexible exchange rates has eliminated the rationale for the specific objectives for U.S. trade and current account surpluses announced in 1971.

Of course, it is true that even under floating exchange rates, countries with serious debt service problems may need to be concerned about trade and current account positions in order to maintain credit-worthiness and minimize the reallocation costs involved in the projected changing of net positions on capital and debt service accounts. But this is hardly a consideration relevant at present to countries like the United States, West Germany, and Japan. Indeed, given the large aggregate current account deficits of oil-importing countries resulting from the oil price increases, current account deficits by the financially strong countries would facilitate improvements of current account positions of countries of less certain credit-worthiness and thereby contribute to a more stable overall world payments problem. In the same way, actions to generate a U.S. current account surplus were necessary for continuation of the Bretton Woods system, not just from the standpoint of U.S. balance-of-payments policy in isolation, but also from the more general standpoint of achieving better balance in the pattern of world payments and greater stability in the international monetary system.

The concern expressed in 1971 over the deterioration in the U.S. trade balance was not only because it contributed to the unsatisfactory overall balance-of-payments position of the United States, but also because it resulted in part from what was widely considered an unfair overvaluation of the dollar and from trade practices abroad. This latter consideration was strongly emphasized by advocates of protectionist trade measures like the Burke-Hartke bill. In such discussions, the actual aggregate quantitative employment effects from overvaluation of the dollar were greatly exaggerated. For instance, contrary to frequent popular assertions, estimates by Lawrence Krause indicated that the decline in the traditional U.S. trade surplus to a deficit position in 1971 could account for only about one-tenth of the increase in unemployment in 1971.[29] Likewise, discussions of the export of American jobs generally failed to distinguish between transitional problems of adjustment to changing trade patterns and longer run employment issues. In other words, a job lost to import competition was a job lost, whether the worker in question soon found another position or not. The limited truth in the concern about the trade balance and domestic employment is often misapplied and exaggerated.[30]

---

[29] Lawrence B. Krause, "How Much of Current Unemployment Did We Import?" *Brookings Papers on Economic Activity*, no. 2 (1971), pp. 417–28.

[30] On this point, see Thomas D. Willett, "International Trade Theory Is Still Relevant," *Banca Nazionale del Lavoro Quarterly Review*, no. 98 (September 1971), pp. 276–92.

Protests of damage from a trade deficit per se are particularly groundless where an increase in imports relative to exports is the result of a domestic boom in economic activity. The current movement in U.S. trade accounts from surplus to deficit is primarily of this nature and should be welcomed for domestic macroeconomic reasons as contributing to a sustained resurgence of domestic economic activity without kindling inflationary pressures. Indeed, from a short-sighted, purely nationalistic standpoint, it could be argued that if market forces did not naturally bring about such a deficit, we should follow deliberate balance-of-payments and exchange rate policies to that end. In a broader context, however, active manipulation of the balance-of-payments accounts for domestic economic purposes would be extremely unwise, for it could easily revive the danger of a breakdown in international financial cooperation and of widespread resort to the ultimately self-defeating, beggar-thy-neighbor policies of the 1930s. For policy purposes, the important point is that a shift of the U.S. trade position from surplus to deficit should not be regarded as an automatic cause for alarm. Indeed under current circumstances such a development would be beneficial from the standpoint both of domestic stabilization policy and of world payments patterns and international financial stability.

This does not mean that we should never be concerned with developments which influence our trade position. U.S. policy may be legitimately concerned if foreign actions such as import barriers and export subsidies represent manipulations to gain unfair competitive advantages. Of course, foreign export subsidies are generally advantageous to domestic consumers, even if they do bring anguish to domestic producers; that is, U.S. consumers are getting goods at less resource cost. Foreign barriers to U.S. exports offer less offsetting advantages to segments of the U.S. economy.

While foreign import restrictions and export subsidies may have the same effects on the trade balances, they generally have opposite effects on our terms of trade.[31] Thus, while both types of foreign manipulations may have the same "unfair" adverse competitive effects on U.S. producers, there are greater offsetting benefits to the United States in the stimulation of foreign exports, suggesting that we should be more concerned about unfair competitive practices that lower our exports than about ones that stimulate our imports. It should be stressed that such concerns are due to particular actions which influence U.S. trade and should be independent of the states of the aggregate surplus or deficit in our trade balance, although

---

[31] See Willett, "International Trade Theory."

domestic political pressures resulting from particular foreign actions may be greater when the overall trade balance is in deficit.

The general point is that while there are many good reasons for being concerned with developments that influence our trade position, there is no sound economic basis for a general presumption that trade surpluses are good and trade deficits are bad. The actual desirability or undesirability of a trade deficit at a particular point in time will depend on many factors, such as the causes of the deficit, its duration, its relation to the state of the domestic economy, the international credit position of the country, et cetera. In many instances, broader considerations would make it unwise to follow active policies to influence the trade balance even if some other trade position might be judged optimal on short-run, national economic criteria alone. In current circumstances, the swing of the U.S. trade balance into deficit as a result of the domestic economic expansion is a desirable development from both domestic and international standpoints.

Postscript: The New IMF Guidelines on Surveillance over Exchange Rate Policies

Shortly after this study was completed, the executive board of the International Monetary Fund reached agreement on a new set of guidelines for surveillance over exchange rate policies. These new guidelines, which are reproduced in Appendix B, replace the 1974 IMF guidelines for floating which were discussed in this chapter. The new guidelines remove or weaken the aspects of the 1974 guidelines which were criticized above and are quite consistent with the general approach to surveillance advocated above.

5

SUMMARY AND
CONCLUSIONS

This study has sought to review the changing attitudes toward exchange rate flexibility from pre-Bretton Woods to the present and to evaluate the performance of the current regime of managed floating as the basis for our new international monetary system.

While the actual operation of floating rates has fallen short of textbook ideals, their performance has been still further removed from the disaster predicted by many critics. On balance, floating rates have served us well and have demonstrated that they form a sound foundation for our international monetary system. The adoption of floating rates has not solved all of our international monetary problems, but in general, it has made such problems less difficult to deal with. It was the pressure of mounting international financial crises which forced the abandonment of par values in the early 1970s, but it was reasoned analysis which led to ratification of floating rates as the new basis for our international monetary system.

The Jamaica Agreements substantially modified the procedures of the Bretton Woods system, but their essential purpose was the preservation and strengthening of the basic principles of international financial cooperation, which were the real heart of the postwar international monetary order established at Bretton Woods. Support for the new international monetary arrangements has not been universal, however. There have been criticisms of the Jamaica Agreements on the grounds that they represent a failure of reform and that they leave us with an international monetary structure that is seriously incomplete and inadequate. The Jamaica Agreements do mark the failure of a particular type of reform, namely the creation of a new par value system based on "stable but adjustable parities." Many had seen this as the major task of the C-20 reform negotiations which were initiated after the breakdown of the par value system in 1971.

This view is reflected in the *Outline of Reform* published in 1974. But as was discussed in chapter 3, attempts to reform the system along these lines had already failed by the time the *Outline of Reform* was published, and for good reasons. The truth in many of these criticisms is that the Jamaica Agreements provide a woefully inadequate basis on which to attempt to restore some form of par value system; but this is not their purpose.

Many have not yet recognized how fundamentally the adoption of a generalized system of floating exchange rates alters the nature of the international confidence and liquidity problems from what it was under the par value system. There are still important issues with respect to the control of international liquidity under our new flexible exchange rate system, but many contemporary discussions of these issues are seriously flawed by the failure to distinguish consistently between par value and floating rate systems and the use of false analogies between domestic and international monetary and liquidity theory.

Official borrowings from the private international financial markets may, but need not, imply a loss of international control over official liquidity creation and use. The best way to improve effective control of international liquidity is through international surveillance of the adjustment process on a country-by-country basis, rather than by focusing primarily on the behavior of international reserve aggregates and attempting to restore some form of official convertibility or asset settlement.

Techniques of multilateral surveillance of the adjustment process will in turn have to be developed by means of a case-history approach, rather than be promulgated in a long list of specific guidelines for target zones, or reference rates, or current account targets. Many have expressed fears that under floating exchange rates, in the absence of detailed international regulations, nations would quickly fall prey to temptations to follow beggar-thy-neighbor policies and that a degeneration into 1930s type economic warfare would soon result. Experience has shown, however, that international financial cooperation is not tied to a specific set of exchange rate procedures. Even the extremely trying circumstances surrounding the collapse of the par value system and adoption of floating exchange rates did not cause the breakdown in cooperation that many had feared. Experience has also indicated that for purposes of limiting manipulative or beggar-thy-neighbor policies, most major countries in practice would rather give more weight to the views of others than cede formal sovereignty or authority to international organizations. Thus, continual judgmental multilateral surveillance seems likely to be more effective than establishment of a large number of specific regulations for balance-of-payments and exchange rate behavior. Any detailed regulations on which formal acceptance could be obtained would probably yield much looser international surveillance than can be accomplished by less formal oversight, based on the types of considerations enumerated in the new IMF guidelines on surveillance of exchange rate policies.

An alternative approach is a system of reference rates to limit permissible intervention behavior. This approach has considerable intellectual attraction. Such a system turns the par value system on its head and specifies when national authorities should not intervene, rather than when they should. This approach suffers from two major difficulties, however. First, it runs the danger of being converted into a target zone approach as authorities respond to pressures to defend their reference rate zone, rather than just avoiding intervention inconsistent with reference rate guidelines. Second, both the reference rate and target zone approaches are based on the assumption that international experts and/or national authorities are able to determine equilibrium exchange rates and to adjust their reference points when equilibrium rates change.

As was discussed in chapter 4, while the reserve indicator approach assumes the market works sufficiently well on average so that persistent one-sided official intervention would suggest manipulation, the target zone and reference rate approaches implicitly assume that officially set targets will, on average, be better indicators of equilibrium exchange rates than are the signals from the private market. It is not necessary to believe naively that the market is always right to see that the latter assumption is an extremely dubious basis for international surveillance of the adjustment process.

There will clearly be occasions when particular countries may want to "take a view" on their exchange rate for a given period, and at such times it is certainly appropriate for other countries and international authorities to want to exercise surveillance over such policies. In such instances, informal expressions of views about an appropriate reference zone for the country in question may be in order. This is quite a different matter, however, from attempting to negotiate, and constantly revise, an international set of reference rates for all major currencies. It is unlikely that the latter course would be an effective use of the scarce resources available—both technical and diplomatic—for the multilateral surveillance of the adjustment process.

The case-history approach to multilateral surveillance undoubtedly will not remove all sources of tension from the operation of the adjustment process; in a world of national governments, this would be an unrealistic goal. But our best chance for minimizing such tensions appears to be the combination of flexible exchange rates and a strong process of multilateral surveillance through the IMF, supplemented by the activities of the OECD working party on balance-of-payments adjustment (WP3) and frequent consultations among high officials of the major countries.

As was discussed in the last section of chapter 4, one of the most important contributions to reducing conflicts among national policies would be broader recognition that trade or current account surpluses are not necessarily prerequisites for domestic economic prosperity. We have come a long way since the misguided battle for trade surpluses that contributed so much to the worldwide economic devastation of the 1930s. But in pluralistic societies, protectionist pressures are never permanently defeated and we must maintain continual vigilance to keep them in check. While many of the practices established at Bretton Woods have been changed drastically because of increased technical knowledge and the evolution of the world economy, the basic philosophy of Bretton Woods, stressing liberal economic policies and international financial cooperation rather than protectionism and autarky, remains as valid and important today as it was in 1944.

APPENDIX A

OECD Forecasts of Trade and Current
Account Balances: 1969–1975

The OECD *Economic Outlook* provides a useful series of forecasts, estimated actual values, and revised actual values of trade and current account balances. The following tables present the forecasts and revised actual values, and the absolute difference between them for seven countries (the United States, the United Kingdom, France, Germany, Italy, Canada, and Japan) from 1969 to 1975.

Table A-1

OECD FORECASTS, 1969 TO 1975
ABSOLUTE DIFFERENCE BETWEEN FORECAST
AND REVISED ACTUAL VALUES
(in millions of dollars, current)

	Mean	Maximum (year)	Minimum (year)
Trade Balance (Annual)			
US	6,066	18,233 (1975)	290 (1970)
UK	2,028	6,909 (1974)	61 (1969)
FRANCE	1,954	5,928 (1975)	28 (1972)
GERMANY	2,654	7,228 (1973)	19 (1971)
ITALY	2,418	5,195 (1975)	241 (1970)
CANADA	698	1,977 (1970)	219 (1972)
JAPAN	1,885	4,562 (1973)	163 (1970)
Current Account Balance (Annual)			
US	6,246	19,150 (1975)	1,056 (1970)
UK	1,966	5,765 (1974)	190 (1970)
FRANCE	2,281	6,528 (1975)	83 (1972)
GERMANY	2,596	8,609 (1974)	4 (1972)
ITALY	2,758	6,445 (1974)	119 (1969)
CANADA	1,122	3,090 (1975)	85 (1969)
JAPAN	2,205	5,336 (1973)	30 (1970)
Trade Balance (Semi-Annual)			
US	2,933	9,335 (75:I)	64 (70:I)
UK	825	3,223 (74:I)	3 (69:I)
FRANCE	873	4,224 (75:I)	6 (72:I)
GERMANY	1,416	4,302 (75:II)	26 (71:I)
ITALY	1,075	3,990 (75:I)	52 (69:I)
CANADA	430	1,023 (70:II)	37 (71:I)
JAPAN	1,185	3,302 (74:II)	30 (72:II)
Current Account Balance (Semi-Annual)			
US	2,841	9,324 (75:I)	254 (69:II)
UK	783	2,520 (74:I)	26 (70:II)
FRANCE	994	4,170 (75:I)	9 (72:II)
GERMANY	1,237	4,736 (74:I)	65 (70:II)
ITALY	1,270	3,960 (75:I)	57 (70:II)
CANADA	414	997 (70:II)	3 (73:II)
JAPAN	1,328	4,075 (73:II)	58 (70:I)

Table A-2
OECD CURRENT ACCOUNT BALANCE FIGURES, ANNUAL

(in millions of dollars, customs basis)

	United States			United Kingdom			Italy		
	Forecast	Revised Actual	Absolute Difference	Forecast	Revised Actual	Absolute Difference	Forecast	Revised Actual	Absolute Difference
1969	1800	− 885	2685	650	998	348	2250	2369	119
1970	1500	444	1056	1200	1390	190	1800	814	986
1971	2000	−2848	4848	800	2536	1736	1250	1846	596
1972	−4000	−8351	4351	600	216	384	2900	2548	352
1973	−5500	513	6013	− 500	−3109	2609	3200	−2418	5618
1974	5000	621a	5621	−3000	−8765	5765	−1350	−7795	6445
1975	−7500	11650	19150	−6500	−3767	2733	−5750	− 554	5196

	France			Germany			Canada			Japan		
	Forecast	Revised Actual	Absolute Difference	Forecast	Revised Actual	Absolute Difference	Forecast	Revised Actual	Absolute Difference	Forecast	Revised Actual	Absolute Difference
1969	− 200	−1400	1200	1800	1604	196	− 650	− 735	85	650	2119	1469
1970	200	− 152	352	400	680	280	− 750	1103	1835	2000	1970	30
1971	− 200	449	649	1350	167	1183	800	341	459	2400	5797	3397
1972	200	283	83	400	396	4	−1000	− 682	318	6800	6467	333
1973	1300	− 677	1977	−1100	4539	5639	− 800	− 427	373	5200	− 136	5336
1974	− 800	−5981	5181	1000	9609	8609	0	−1680	1680	− 500	−4693	4193
1975	−6250	278	6528	6000	3734	2266	−3750	− 660	3090	0	− 680	680

a Excluding Indian rupee cancellation and other extraordinary grants.

OECD Forecasts of Trade and Current Account Balances: Notes

(1) Data are reported on a customs basis by value, millions of current dollars, seasonally adjusted.

(2) Annual and first-half forecasts are taken from the country pages of the December issue of *Economic Outlook*; for example, the 1972 and 1972:I forecasts are taken from the December 1971 issue.

(3) Second-half forecasts are taken from the July issue; for example, the 1972:II forecasts come from the July 1972 issue.

(4) The 1968 forecasts, however, come from the July 1968 issue; including the annual and first-half figures.

(5) Estimates of actual annual values are taken from the country pages of the December issue of *Economic Outlook*; for example, the estimated actual annual values for 1972 are taken from the December 1972 issue.

(6) Estimates of actual first-half values are taken from the July issue; for example, the estimated values for 1972:I come from the July 1972 issue.

(7) Estimates of actual second-half values come from the December issue; for example, estimates for 1972:II come from the December 1972 issue.

(8) Revised estimates of annual, first-half, and second-half values are all taken from the December issue, one year after the value date; for example, 1972, 1972:I, 1972:II revised estimates are taken from the December 1973 issue.

(9) Because of the changes in the par value system, both the July and the December issues of 1973 report trade balances in SDRs. Dollar–SDR ratios have been derived by dividing the $billion current account forecast for each country, found on page 56 of the December 1973 issue and on page 35 of the July 1973 issue, by the corresponding SDR billion figure found on the same page.

APPENDIX B

International Monetary Fund Executive Board Decision on Surveillance over Exchange Rate Policies, April 29, 1977

1.   The Executive Board has discussed the implementation of Article IV of the proposed second amendment of the Articles of Agreement and has approved the attached document entitled *Surveillance over Exchange Rate Policies*. The Fund shall act in accordance with this document when the second amendment becomes effective. In the period before that date the Fund shall continue to conduct consultations in accordance with present procedures and decisions.

2.   The Fund shall review the document entitled *Surveillance over Exchange Rate Policies* at intervals of two years and at such other times as consideration of it is placed on the agenda of the Executive Board.

General Principles

Article IV, Section 3(a) provides that "The Fund shall oversee the international monetary system in order to ensure its effective operation, and shall oversee the compliance of each member with its obligations under Section 1 of this Article." Article IV, Section 3(b) provides that in order to fulfill its functions under 3(a), "the Fund shall exercise firm surveillance over the exchange rate policies of members, and shall adopt specific principles for the guidance of all members with respect to those policies." Article IV, Section 3(b) also provides that "The principles adopted by the Fund shall be consistent with cooperative arrangements by which members maintain the value of their currencies in relation to the value of the currency or currencies of other members, as well as with other exchange arrangements of a member's choice consistent with the purposes of the Fund and Section 1 of this Article. These principles shall respect the domestic social

143

and political policies of members, and in applying these principles the Fund shall pay due regard to the circumstances of members." In addition, Article IV, Section 3(b) requires that "Each member shall provide the Fund with the information necessary for such surveillance, and, when requested by the Fund, shall consult with it on the member's exchange rate policies."

The principles and procedures set out below, which apply to all members whatever their exchange arrangements and whatever their balance-of-payments position, are adopted by the Fund in order to perform its functions under Section 3(b). They are not necessarily comprehensive and are subject to reconsideration in the light of experience. They do not deal directly with the Fund's responsibilities referred to in Section 3(a), although it is recognized that there is a close relationship between domestic and international economic policies. This relationship is emphasized in Article IV which includes the following provision: Recognizing . . . that a principal objective (of the international monetary system) is the continuing development of the orderly underlying conditions that are necessary for financial and economic stability, each member undertakes to collaborate with the Fund and other members to assure orderly exchange arrangements and to promote a stable system of exchange rates."

Principles for the Guidance of Members' Exchange Rate Policies

A. A member shall avoid manipulating exchange rates or the international monetary system in order to prevent effective balance-of-payments adjustment or to gain an unfair competitive advantage over other members.

B. A member should intervene in the exchange market if necessary to counter disorderly conditions which may be characterized *inter alia* by disruptive short-term movements in the exchange value of its currency.

C. Members should take into account in their intervention policies the interests of other members, including those of the countries in whose currencies they intervene.

Principles of Fund Surveillance over Exchange Rate Policies

1. The surveillance of exchange rate policies shall be adapted to the needs of international adjustment as they develop. The functioning of the international adjustment process shall be kept under review by the Executive Board and Interim Committee and the assess-

ment of its operation shall be taken into account in the implementation of the principles set forth below.

2. In its surveillance of the observance by members of the principles set forth above, the Fund shall consider the following developments as among those which might indicate the need for discussion with a member:

 (i) protracted large-scale intervention in one direction in the exchange market;

 (ii) an unsustainable level of official or quasi-official borrowing, or excessive and prolonged short-term official or quasi-official lending, for balance-of-payments purposes;

 (iii) (a) the introduction, substantial intensification, or prolonged maintenance, for balance-of-payments purposes, of restrictions on, or incentives for, current transactions or payments, or

  (b) the introduction or substantial modification for balance-of-payments purposes of restrictions on, or incentives for, the inflow or outflow of capital;

 (iv) the pursuit, for balance-of-payments purposes, of monetary and other domestic financial policies that provide abnormal encouragement or discouragement to capital flows; and

 (v) behavior of the exchange rate that appears to be unrelated to underlying economic and financial conditions including factors affecting competitiveness and long-term capital movements.

3. The Fund's appraisal of a member's exchange rate policies shall be based on an evaluation of the developments in the member's balance of payments against the background of its reserve position and its external indebtedness. This appraisal shall be made within the framework of a comprehensive analysis of the general economic situation and economic policy strategy of the member, and shall recognize that domestic as well as external policies can contribute to timely adjustment of the balance of payments. The appraisal shall take into account the extent to which the policies of the member, including its exchange rate policies, serve the objectives of the continuing development of the orderly underlying conditions that are necessary for financial stability, the promotion of sustained sound economic growth, and reasonable levels of employment.

Procedures for Surveillance

1. Each member shall notify the Fund in appropriate detail within thirty days after the Second Amendment becomes effective of the exchange arrangements it intends to apply in fulfillment of its

obligations under Article IV, Section 1. Each member shall also notify the Fund promptly of any changes in its exchange arrangements.

2.   Members shall consult with the Fund regularly under Article IV. The consultations under Article IV shall comprehend the regular consultations under Articles VIII and XIV. In principle such consultations shall take place annually, and shall include consideration of the observance by members of the principles set forth above as well as of a member's obligations under Article IV, Section 1. Not later than three months after the termination of discussions between the member and the staff, the Executive Board shall reach conclusions and thereby complete the consultation under Article IV.

3.   Broad developments in exchange rates will be reviewed periodically by the Executive Board, *inter alia* in discussions of the international adjustment process within the framework of the World Economic Outlook. The Fund will continue to conduct special consultations in preparing for these discussions.

4.   The Managing Director shall maintain close contact with members in connection with their exchange arrangements and exchange policies, and will be prepared to discuss on the initiative of a member important changes that it contemplates in its exchange arrangements or its exchange rate policies.

5.   If, in the interval between Article IV consultations, the Managing Director, taking into account any views that may have been expressed by other members, considers that a member's exchange rate policies may not be in accord with the exchange rate principles, he shall raise the matter informally and confidentially with the member, and shall conclude promptly whether there is a question of the observance of the principles. If he concludes that there is such a question, he shall initiate and conduct on a confidential basis a discussion with the member under Article IV, Section 3(b). As soon as possible after the completion of such a discussion, and in any event not later than four months after its initiation, the Managing Director shall report to the Executive Board on the results of the discussion. If, however, the Managing Director is satisfied that the principles are being observed, he shall informally advise all Executive Directors, and the staff shall report on the discussion in the context of the next Article IV consultation; but the Managing Director shall not place the matter on the agenda of the Executive Board unless the member requests that this procedure be followed.

6.   The Executive Directors shall review annually the general implementation of the Fund's surveillance over members' exchange rate policies.

Cover and book design: Pat Taylor